THE RIGHT TRUE END OF LOVE

For Frances, who is …

Stephen R. White

The right true end of love

SEXUALITY AND THE CONTEMPORARY CHURCH

the columba press

First published in 2005 by
the columba press
55A Spruce Avenue, Stillorgan Industrial Park,
Blackrock, Co Dublin

Cover by Bill Bolger
Origination by The Columba Press
Printed in Ireland by Betaprint Ltd, Dublin

ISBN 1 85607 484 6

Table of Contents

columba

Review Slip

Title   The Right True End Of Love

Subtitle   Sexuality and the Contemporary Church

Author   Stephen R. White

ISBN   1-85607-484-6

Price   €12.99/£9.50

Extent   143pp

Publisher Columba

For further information contact:
Ciara Doorley,
Marketing Assistant
Columba, 55A Stillorgan Industrial Park, Blackrock,
Co Dublin, Ireland.
Tel + 353 1 294 2556 ext 222
Fax + 353 1 294 2564   Email ciara@columba.ie

'The history of Christianity's inhumanity is a history of betrayal of faith, of refusal to recognise the divine in the human other.'
— Enda McDonagh, *Vulnerable to the Holy*,
Dublin: The Columba Press, 2004, p 65

Whoever loves, if he do not propose the right true end of love,
he's one that goes to sea for nothing but to make him sick.
— John Donne, *Elegies*, 'Love's Progress'

For the love of God is broader
Than the measures of man's mind,
And the heart of the Eternal
Is most wonderfully kind.

But we make his love too narrow
By false limits of our own;
And we magnify his strictness
With a zeal he will not own.
— Frederick W. Faber, *Souls of men, why will ye scatter*

Introduction

Sexuality is high on the church's agenda at present, in a myriad of forms both positive and negative. Hardly a single issue of a church journal (of any denomination) goes past but it contains at least one article or letter on some aspect of sexuality: indeed an entire volume of the Church of Ireland journal *Search* has recently been devoted exclusively to the subject. Beyond this, the church is structurally and institutionally beset by the topic at the moment, whether negatively in having to come to terms with clerical sexual abuse in all of its forms, or more positively in the production of bishops' statements, Doctrine Commission reports and pastoral encyclicals which try realistically to come to grips with one or another aspect of the subject, to say nothing of the recent *Windsor Report*, of which more in due course.

In this volume I propose – without downplaying the church's need to come to terms with, and make amends for its sad history of sexual abuse – to concentrate exclusively on efforts to interpret and define the church's stance for the future on the issues surrounding human sexuality. These efforts are worthy indeed, but they seem to me, in their institutional manifestations at least, to be too cautious, too unimaginative, too 'samey' and too ultimately untheologically based to be of any lasting significance. What it boils down to is that they are all eminently ignorable – delicately balanced and nuanced statements which promise to 'listen' to the experience and views of certain groups, but which effectively uphold the *status quo* almost unquestioningly. A pastoral statement issued in 2003 by the Irish House of Bishops is a case in point – in two and a half startlingly dull pages it succeeds in saying absolutely nothing which is at all meaningful. Indeed, on dutifully reading it out in my various churches, the

comments about it have ranged merely from 'nonsense' to 'rub-
bish'. The time has come to explore Christian attitudes to sexuality, and especially, but not exclusively, homosexuality, from a
different and more dynamic viewpoint, and to discover theologically soundly based means by which our understanding of
Christian ethics can be constructively re-thought.

Even to attempt this is a daunting task, but it is equally a necessary one. Essentially the most significant single problem with
the sort of church pronouncements on sexuality outlined above
is that they all begin (and effectively end) with the premise that
particular expressions of sexuality are right or wrong – and this
applies in principle even when we have not yet decided which
of these options is in fact the case. The presupposition is that
somehow right and wrong are the central reference points.

And there are two difficulties with this approach. The first is
the question of how we actually decide what is right and wrong
(of which more in Chapter Five), and the second is that the concepts of right and wrong are often *a priori* assumptions which
fail to ask the question as to *why* things are right and wrong, and
which equally fail to explain how any particular conception of
morality fits in with our doctrinal scheme of things.

Thus, it will be argued, a different starting point – and consequently a very different vision of and for Christian ethics – is
necessary. As we have already argued, ethics can not be done in
a vacuum, and indeed there is a crucial sense in which, strange
though it undoubtedly sounds, the necessary starting point for
ethics is not, in fact, ethics, but doctrine and metaphysics. This
has always been the case, but even with this acknowledgement
Christianity has all too often fallen foul of the Scylla of God as
moral being on one side and the Charybdis of reified morality
on the other. Thus, in the first case, there is the danger that we
decide what God approves of on the basis of our own moral
choices, whether acknowledged or unacknowledged; and in the
other case the danger is that whatever morality is put in place
comes, eventually, to have a higher standing than (and one
which becomes totally independent of) God himself.

The channel between these two hazards is admittedly narrow, but what seems to be required is a renewed exploration of who God is, metaphysically, conceptually and experientially, which will then inform our understanding of what God wills, and therefore of what we will come to describe (although as we shall see again in Chapter Five, there is a vital intermediate step before this) as being 'right' or 'wrong'. The contention of this study is that traditional metaphysics (and consequently much of ethics) has frequently been less than helpful in the realm of human sexuality, and that both need to be substantially re-thought. It is the hope of this study that in the light of this re-think a new and more dynamic and creative understanding of God and ethics (and therefore of sexuality) may emerge. Success in this endeavour may be a different matter, but the need for an attempt is growing more urgent by the day.

CHAPTER ONE

Sex and the City of God

In May 2003 I attended – and chaired a session at – the 39th Glenstal Ecumenical Conference, the theme of which was: 'Inclining the Ear of the Heart: Voices on Love, Sexuality and Friendship'. At one level this conference has turned out to be highly topical, given the recent election of two openly homosexual bishops – one an American diocesan and the other an English suffragan – and the consequent (and predictable) furore surrounding these appointments and the subsequent withdrawal of acceptance of nomination by one of them.

However, transient topicality was not the reason why such a theme was chosen for the conference, fortuitous though it may have been for the general level of interest aroused and levels of participation which resulted. Far more important, though, was the conviction that the conference was addressing an issue of critical relevance for the present time. Thus, regardless of episcopal elections and appointments, the church and the churches are entering a crucial period in the area of human relationships, a period of much soul-searching, of potential change, of possible crisis and division.

The questions at issue are legion – and all of them impinge upon our deepest understandings of what it means to be human, to be embodied, to be sexual beings, to have a sense of self-worth and self-identity and so on. To take a few examples almost at random: should openly homosexual people be ordained, let alone consecrated as bishops? Should same-sex unions be able to be blessed by the church? Should same-sex couples be entitled to adopt and raise children together? Should sexual intimacy and intercourse be restricted to lifelong heterosexual marriage? Should our physical nature and desires be merely tolerated or should they be celebrated by us in the church? Should *agape* continue to be exalted as a higher love than *eros*? Is our human embodied love (including sexual love) an expression of and reflection of divine love or not?

That the churches are even debating such issues is itself encouraging, but potentially even more serious and disturbing, especially for the more traditionally-minded, is the unpalatable fact that such discussions ultimately reach beyond their initial starting points and reach into the heart of Christian doctrine itself, and simultaneously to the heart of Christian ethics, leaving former certainties uncertain, and apparently safe pastures full of unexploded doctrinal, pastoral and ethical land mines.

The reasons why this is so are immensely complex, but essentially they are five in number, although all are to varying degrees related, and all have a common core in the extent to which traditional Christian doctrine and ethics succeeds – and may even be designed to this end – in making those who do not totally conform to the established pattern of orthodoxy and orthopraxis feel both marginalised and guilty.

The first is simply that we are plunged into this situation by virtue of the rapid and almost complete breakdown of the familiar system of doctrinal and ethical norms, obedience and even control, upon which the church has relied so successfully for so many centuries in order to enforce its beliefs and practices. Thus, throughout much of the last two thousand years, or at least since Constantine embraced Christianity, the values of church and society have been largely coterminous. For much of that period, indeed, they have been explicitly linked as church and state walked more or less hand in hand in the business of government. Since, perhaps, the Enlightenment, and then increasingly throughout the Victorian era and the early twentieth century, there has been a growing separation between the two, although one might nonetheless argue that, in spite of the progressive secularisation of society, it was still governed (morally speaking) on many of the traditional Christian principles, even if the state and many individual members of it no longer formally espoused the faith of their forbears.

Even this lingering 'flavour' of secular Christian-derived ethics has now departed, and religious and moral attitudes have changed with ever greater rapidity over the last fifty years or so, such that our contemporary world is now filled with as many religious and ethical options as one could possibly want, so much so that it has more than once been described as a *smorgasbord* culture in which one simply conducts a 'pick and mix' exercise from among the many bits and pieces which appeal most.

What, so far then, has been the church's response to this changed situation? On the whole it has certainly not been one which has found much to rejoice over in this 'brave new world' of moral freedom. Admittedly there have been those radicals who have celebrated this loosening of the age-old stranglehold of traditional Christian ethics on society, but for the most part the church, whether evangelical or high church, has tended to draw in its horns and lay down its own 'standards' with a new intensity in the face of the apparent laxity of the vast bulk of modern society.

Essentially this has been – and is being – done in one of two ways, depending upon the degree of institutionalism attached to any particular church or group, but the effect is much the same whichever path is taken. In the more institutionalised churches, therefore, the response has been to issue directives from some central source, the prime example of which would be the Roman Catholic Church with its stream of encyclicals emanating from the pope and the curia. More loosely structured churches do not usually have any similar mechanism, and in this case conformity is likely to be imposed simply by an increasingly conservative and exclusive peer-pressure mechanism – to belong one must subscribe to certain views and uphold certain 'standards'. For the individual who differs in either of these two forms of church life there are two choices: one can decide either to become unchurched and free to hold more liberal views which the world outside the church will more willingly endorse than the church itself would, or one can remain churched but find oneself overtly or covertly (depending on how public one's views become) not approved of by that church. And if this is true of those who only think in certain ways, then it is inevitably even more true of those who actually behave in ways which are contrary to the governing mentality and norms. As attitudes harden in the face of a changing moral climate, it is all too easy for the supposedly all-embracing church to become a place and a community where some are seen as 'deviant' and are thereby made to feel guilty simply for being who they are.

The second reason for the difficulties of the present debate is the vast distance which the church is going to have to travel if it is going to redeem the situation of guilt inducement and exclusion which we have outlined above. It is even going to have to alter its view of what constitutes an adequate response to such groups as homosexuals. At present the most eirenic and charitable goal, even among most of those who wish attitudes to change at all, is toleration. It is a spirit of toleration which breathes so vapidly through the more charitable of the Lambeth Conference resolutions and through various episcopal and working party reports on human sexuality.

Toleration of difference, though, is by no means the same thing as celebration of difference, either in what it feels like to be the recipient of it or in the mind-set which it induces in the purveyor of it. As one participant at Glenstal put it very powerfully: 'Don't tolerate me! I don't want to be tolerated and I don't like being tolerated! Relate to me – like me or loath me, but don't just tolerate me!' And he was right. Toleration as an end point is not acceptable, for it does not lead to a full acceptance of, and real celebration of difference. Instead it is inclined to take on the flavour of being a favour graciously conferred by the 'normal' majority on a somehow 'inadequate' minority – and of course it is also quite possible to tolerate something (or, more particularly, someone) apparently at least, whilst still in fact being disapproving of those who differ.

The third problem for the church (and for those who feel

themselves to be on the wrong end of church teaching) arises
from another set of double standards similar in many ways to
those involved in the toleration versus celebration of difference
issue. That is, the church's 'official' position on many issues concerning sexuality is different from that which many otherwise
faithful and 'obedient' priests and lay people are attempting to
live out. Thus there is an ever-widening gulf between church
teaching and much of grass roots church practice, and the result
is a residual guilt in many people which is all the more intolerable in that all that they are attempting to do is to live out the
gospel command of 'love your neighbour as yourself' in ways
which seem relevant to their (and their neighbour's) situation.

To move away from homosexuality then – although it remains, as Glenstal demonstrated, central to the church's attitude
to contemporary ethical thinking – a prime example would be
the issue of contraception within the Roman Catholic Church.
'On the ground' the church (in the guise of a myriad parish
priests) has begun to accept and condone – and perhaps even
moving beyond such toleration, has begun even to rejoice in and
celebrate – expressions of human sexuality which do not have
procreation as their explicit goal. At the same time, however, the
'official' Roman Catholic Church line is that all such non-procreative sexual activity is sinful, and the result is one of two
responses, either of which is damaging to the church. These are
either a guilty admission of continuing membership or an outright rejection of a church which appears to be ethically still in
the stone age. So too, to return to our central issue, with homosexuality. Individual lay people (and even priests) may affirm
and value homosexual individuals and couples, but the church
officially continues to condemn, and it is hard to see what alternative responses are available to Christian homosexuals at present other than a guilt-ridden church membership or an increasingly disillusioned rejection of their faith and church.

Indeed, and it is the fourth problem which the church has to
face and deal with, this dichotomy between guilty adherence to
the church and disillusioned rejection of it seems to apply all too

often to all expressions of human sexuality – even those such as heterosexual marriage, which the church does its official best to approve of!

In a very real sense this goes back to the distinction between toleration and celebration which was raised earlier, and the church's response to the fact of human sexuality appears most often to stem from the former rather than from the latter. Having spoken somewhat critically of Roman Catholic attitudes to sexuality in connection with contraception, I propose here to 'balance the books' and draw all of my illustrations from within my own church family, that of Anglicanism, and specifically from within my adopted branch of that family, the Church of Ireland.

The Church of Ireland, of course, is trying hard to be contemporary, relevant and forward looking: but where, with grim regularity does it refer to for its sense of identity and its (often literally) governing rules? The answer is the *Book of Common Prayer*, by which is meant all of the various revisions and reprintings stemming from the 1662 book, rather than the 2004 *Book of Common Prayer* which includes also services in contemporary language. And what does the *Book of Common Prayer* (even in its more moderate revised Irish form) have to say about the reasons and rationale for heterosexual marriage? Apparently, marriage was ordained:

> First, for the increase of mankind, according to the will of God, and for the due ordering of families and households, that children might be brought up in the fear and nurture of the Lord, and to the praise of his holy Name;
> Secondly, for the hallowing of the union betwixt man and woman, and for the avoidance of sin;
> Thirdly, for the mutual society, help and comfort, that the one ought to have of the other, both in prosperity and adversity.

I have lost count of the number of times that a wedding couple and I have shared a somewhat regretful laugh at the church's negativity and topsy-turviness with regard to the reasons for marriage. Admittedly, of course, some of the reasons for this explanation of marriage are historical and much of this may have sounded generally acceptable in the seventeenth century – although this does not necessarily mean that it was right even then. Today, however, such an outline of the rationale for marriage should be given a decent burial for at least two main reasons.

First, it is, according to most understandings of marriage, back to front, placing the having and rearing of children first and the couple's own relationship last. Children may well be important to many couples, but they are not the primary focus of marriage – couples marry because they love one another, and it is, logically and practically, out of that prior love that children come. Furthermore – and in keeping with our remarks on the official Roman Catholic attitude to contraception – the placing of children first simply pre-empts any discussion on the role and value of non-procreative sex and the importance of the sexual relationship within marriage for the strengthening and enriching of the marriage bond without immediate reference to children.

This leads directly to the second problem with this rationale for marriage – its utter negativity regarding sexuality. Marriage is ordained not for the joy and delight of sexual union but for the 'avoidance of sin'. In other words, the flavour which comes across most powerfully is, 'If you can't manage to do without sex, then you had at least better get married'! Such an implicit message is damaging both to the church and to the individual couple – although responses to it have changed over the centuries. In the past, one suspects, many couples lived lives either of sexual repression or of interiorised guilt (because they actually had the temerity to enjoy sex) in deference to church teaching. Today, far more couples are likely to reject the church's attitude to sex altogether (and with it quite possibly the church itself), which must surely weaken the church's attempts to have any positive moral input into the ordering of society and family.

Admittedly the church has made strenuous efforts – liturgically at least – to move away from this negative perception of human sexuality. Thus the 1984 *Alternative Prayer Book* marriage service completely re-writes the purposes of marriage: it begins from the couple's own relationship of love and affection, proceeds to the sexual expression of this love ('... that they may know each other in love, and through the joy of their bodily union they may strengthen the union of their hearts and lives'), and moves from this to the potential fruit of that love in the procreation of children. And yet ... and yet ... even still today this comes across all too often as a toleration of, rather than a celebration of human sexual love. Yes, these are the words of the actual service, but how often, in marriage preparation courses, in general church teaching and so on, is full justice done to the sheer joy and delight of totally committed sexual union? The words may be there in the marriage service, and the outside world may have come to approve of human sexuality, but the church – especially when one considers its comments on any form of unmarried love – all too often still seems merely to be in the business of the 'avoidance of sin' rather than that of a celebration of life and love. The result of this, still today, is that many (most?) people who attend church at all still feel at some level bad about their sexuality – and probably in direct proportion to their church commitment!

Once again, this leads directly to the fifth and final reason why the church (and its decreasingly few faithful) face such problems today in the areas both of doctrine and of ethics, and this is the all-pervasiveness of the church's claims in both of these areas, which, by definition, therefore, may lead to an equally all-pervasive good or all-pervasive bad – or indeed any station in between.

Thus, not only in terms of its explicit or implicit sexual teaching, but also in terms of the church's doctrine as it impinges upon their sense of self-understanding and self-identity, Christians and would-be Christians are being hurt in their very sense of self-worth (including, but not exclusively, their sense of sexual self-worth) by the church's doctrine and teaching. We have seen this already in terms of teaching overtly connected with human sexuality in the marriage service, but this hurtful potential of Christianity is reinforced even at the initially abstract-seeming level of doctrine and metaphysics. Here the issue is perhaps more to do with gender than sexuality, but the two are inevitably linked, and an individual's perception of the significance of gender may well be – although not necessarily – related to their experience of sexuality.

The prime example of this is the church's insistence upon gender related terms for its own understanding of God. As soon as one asks the question, 'Who is God?' within the Christian tradition, one is instantly confronted with a gender-based response: God is the Three Persons of the Trinity, Father, Son, and Holy Spirit.

At this point it is essential to establish that there are two factors at work here. One is the intention of those who framed this expression of doctrine, and the other is the effect which this doctrine has on a fairly substantial minority of believers. And it is important not to impute wrong motives to either group, especially the former, lest the whole issue become beclouded by gender-based slanging matches! Thus, at the outset it should be said that those who first framed the doctrine of the Trinity in these terms were attempting, within the acceptable terms of reference of their own world, to construct an understanding of God which reflected the three emphases of creativity, redemption and indwelling. To deny this would be unfair in the extreme.

The problem, though, is that history – and within that history the power of the Christian church itself – has solidified (or perhaps petrified is a better word) that model of God into an unchanging and supposedly unchangeable definition of God. What was once a helpful model has become an unhelpful idol.

What has happened is in essence very simple. The original framers of doctrine attempted to do pictorial justice to the reality of God as that God was encountered. Over the centuries that picture of God has come to be assumed to be the reality of God and has therefore become inflexible. Thus it may still be today that for many people the image of God as Father is helpful: fathers are loving, comforting, available, reliable and so on. Yet the problem is that this is no longer a picture of God: rather it *is* God, and therefore for those who find the picture unhelpful or even painful there is no available alternative. For such people, a call to faith is a call to painful belief or to an equally painful rejection of belief. For those whose experience of fatherhood is aggressive, repressive or even abusive, the apparent necessity to call God 'Father' is yet one more barrier to belief – all the affirmation and hope which a life of faith might engender is annihilated by the realisation that the deity is only a larger version of that from which they seek deliverance. The net effect of this – and this was borne out by a large number of comments at the Glenstal Conference – is that Christianity and its concepts of God effectively create groups who are full of pain and shame at their own identity. After all, if your relationship with an earthly father is one which produces pain and/or shame, it is hardly surprising that these feelings should travel with you into a faith whose confession begins: 'I believe in God the Father'!

These, then, are among the various problems which confront Christianity in the realm of sexuality and gender at the present time. They are serious problems and potentially destructive both of the faith of the individual Christian or would-be Christian and of the church's sense of cohesion and self-understanding, doctrinally and ethically. In the face of these problems the ultimate question is: 'How can the church today nurture a community of Christians who are at home with and rejoice in themselves, their personalities and bodies, and for whom createdness and sexuality are intrinsically good, and who on the basis of this sense of self-worth are ready to celebrate together and to reach out to others with the warmth of God's loving-kindness which produces in us that joy which Jesus describes as being "full"?'

It is the intention of this book to provide, in outline at least, the beginnings of a doctrinal and ethical response to the problem and answer to the question.

CHAPTER TWO

The Trouble with Metaphysics

One of the corners which the church has resolutely backed itself into over the centuries (and beginning very early on) is the metaphysical one, with the result that human thought and language have tended to impose definition upon God, rather than God being allowed to remain somewhat diffuse and the *mysterium tremendum* beyond language.

For we have a problem when speaking (or more properly, attempting to speak) of God. At one level, this problem is so simple as hardly to need stating, yet at another it is so profound in its consequences (especially when the problem is ignored or unnoticed) that it cannot be stressed too highly. This problem is that, quite simply, it is ultimately impossible for us to speak of God. The Maynooth theologian Martin Henry put it particularly succinctly when he wrote in his aptly-titled book, *On Not Understanding God*, that the only thing that we can say about God is that, 'God is'. Beyond this there is only silence.

The reason for this is not hard to seek. When we speak of God we are, by definition, attempting to encompass and express the infinite within the compass of the finite, and both parts of this exercise are entirely beyond us. Our minds and our thoughts do not and cannot contain the concepts, the ideas, the sheer fullness of life and energy necessary to encompass God and, generated as it is by these same minds, our language equally fails to find adequate expression for the overwhelming reality of that God.

This represents a major problem, certainly, but there are two essential responses to it, one of which leads to an admittedly uncomfortable but probably authentic religious lifestyle, and the other of which (and it has been the majority option throughout the ages) leads to a much more comfortable but inauthentic and frequently damaging religious lifestyle.

One response is to go with the uncomfortable reality of the situation: that we cannot encompass or express God. This involves a number of things. First, it insists upon the admission of human limitation, both in terms of thought and of language. Secondly, it demands the humility of uncertainty: the acknowledgement that in any statement about God (whether concerning God's nature, God's demands or God's activities) we may be entirely wrong. And thirdly, it requires the existentially challenging admission that God actually lives (and acts) beyond all of our formulations, expectations, definitions and so on. We have no handle upon God.

The alternative response is much more comfortable, but it is also false to the nature of God and shallow (though admittedly far easier and cosier) in its spiritual and ethical implications. This is to continue (as even the most ardent adherent of this position would admit we must) to pay lip service to the mystery, majesty and ineffability of God, whilst at the same time in practice actually ignoring this whole dimension of divinity and focusing all of our attention upon the human concepts and language within which we attempt, haltingly, to express something of that divinity. Such an approach is, wittingly or unwittingly, all too common and it leads to two positions, one conservative and one radical, each of which is equally comfortable and equally inauthentic – indeed it is a prime instance of those rare occasions on which the ultra-conservative and the ultra-radical actually share something of the same ground!

For the ultra-radical, therefore, the truth of the matter is that God is only the sum of our human aspirations and ideals anyway, and therefore these are what must govern our metaphysical and ethical thinking – if, indeed, there is any further need for metaphysics at all. The shortcomings of this approach are obvious and have been dealt with by many people (myself included) elsewhere. More insidious, though, is the notion, which tends to creep into ultra-conservatism, that we can know with absolute

certainty what God wills or requires of us, and also know precisely of which things s/he does or does not approve. This allows
our human formulations of that will, requirement or approval to
take on divine proportions simply because we *know* that such
and such is the mind of God. The effect of this, whether inten-
tionally or more probably unintentionally, is to reify the human
and transform it into the divine. Thus our descriptions of God
become (to our way of thinking at least) what God actually *is*,
and we begin to feel that our understanding of God can successfully encompass the divine, whether metaphysically or ethically,
with the consequence, as we shall see, that God is not permitted
to be God and becomes trapped within the realm of human
knowledge and ethics. Something of this sort has happened all
too often in a great deal of religious thinking and it unleashes all
of the very real problems of metaphysics.

These problems stem, as we have indicated, from the fact
that metaphysics is a branch of human reasoning and not, although we may like to think that it is, a means of intellectually
'photocopying' or imaging the reality of God. It is this gap – and
more specifically the all too frequent lack of awareness of it – between human thinking and God's own self which makes for the
difficulties.

It is all very well to start thinking about God, but the rules of
human thought must remain subject to the object of that thought
and not *vice versa*. The difficulty is that in every branch of human
thinking, metaphysics included, a premium is placed upon clarity and logic, and it is these which threaten to supplant divinity.
Thus it has always been said – and presumably correctly – of
God that he cannot do that which is logically impossible, such as
creating a square circle. As far as it goes, this is fine, but there
comes a point at which our perception of logic begins to dictate
the reality of God, such that we come to claim that God cannot
encompass different qualities which, from our limited point of
view, appear diametrically opposed and inconsistent. The point
at issue, however, is that the extension from mathematical logic
(the impossibility of the squared circle) to what one might call

existential logic (qualities of being) is, though itself apparently logical, not in fact justified. We have defined the square and the circle and therefore we are in an excellent position to say that a square circle is both illogical and impossible: we have not, however, defined being, but merely experienced one mode of it (and that a limited one), and we are therefore in no position to prejudge what may be logical or possible within the whole vast realm of being which lies beyond us.

A prime example which will serve to illustrate this issue – and it is one which has bedevilled theologians since time immemorial, as well as having tremendous implications for the rest of our argument – is the question of the passibility or impassibility of God. According to the rules of classical theological metaphysics, the formula for arriving at a conclusion is quite a simple one. To begin with the states of passibility (susceptibility to change and specifically to suffering) and impassibility (the lack of this susceptibility) are assumed, reasonably enough, to be incompatible. God cannot, therefore, logically be both and must, clearly, be one or the other. But which? Unfortunately, in providing its answer, Christianity at this point baptised the wisdom of Plato, Aristotle *et al*. For the classical metaphysicians, suffering was a form of change and change was equivalent to decay (and it is curious, and indicative of how deeply rooted this idea is, to see how it was echoed thousands of years later in the hymn 'Abide with me': 'change and decay in all around I see'). In the light of this, therefore, unchangeableness was the eternal and primary quality, both ontologically and ethically. A passible goodness might in theory be changed away from its own goodness: only an impassible God could be guaranteed to be eternally and unchangeably good, omnipotent and so on. God, therefore, had, by the internal definitions of metaphysics, to be impassible – and God remained lumbered with his impassibility for the best part of the next two thousand years of the Christian tradition.

It is important also to spell out the full implications of the theological and ethical meaning of impassibility. At one level it sounds wonderful to learn that God is unchangeable – a firm centre in a shifting universe. However, the picture begins to look bleaker and less satisfactory when one realises that the primary meaning of impassibility is the inability to suffer, for this makes the concepts of sympathy and empathy very hard indeed to posit of any impassible being. To such a being the suffering of others may be seen as a moral evil to be remedied, but this is an abstract judgement which cannot (if God is impassible) actually impinge upon the heart of God. Taken to its extreme, it is not far from here to Deism and to all forms of religion which have seen God as the 'unmoved mover'.

This doctrine of impassibility, and its unfortunate consequences for the apparent nature of God, is something with which Christianity has struggled to come to terms throughout most of its history. The central dilemma is the incompatibility between a God who is impassible and a God who cares, and it is hard to see how this yawning chasm between the two supposed poles of God's being could ever be satisfactorily bridged within the terms of the classical metaphysical debate. Attempts have always been made, of course, but the result has been that Christianity has teetered on a very high and uneasy tightrope between a God who is remote (because impassible) and a God who somehow, and equally illogically, is supposed to care about us at the same time as being impassible. The metaphysical imperative towards impassibility has been constantly at variance with the lived experience of God who is not only intellectually thought to, but also experientially felt to, care for and be involved with his people.

This is a profound tension and one which has never been – and, I suggest, can never be – satisfactorily resolved. Again plenty of attempts have been made, but credulity or metaphysics or both have usually been stretched to their breaking point in the process. The classical 'solution' to the dilemma involves invoking, in one form or another, the different qualities which may be predicated of the various Persons of the Trinity. Thus it may be argued that God as he is in himself (as 'Father' if you like) is indeed impassible, but that this same God brought his care for humanity into passionate being in the form of the Second Person of the Trinity, his Son, Jesus Christ.

This is a neat and superficially attractive theory for, if one holds that Jesus is indeed the Christ and the Second Person of the Trinity, then there can be no doubt that in Jesus God empathised, suffered, and experienced the passionate nature of embodied human life. However, there are two responses to this: one is that Jesus lived as he did (and suffered as he did) because this truly reflects the nature of God as passionate; and the other is that God remained (and remains) existentially unchanged by the human experience of Jesus. The second of these is the majority verdict of Christianity, and whilst it conveniently champions the traditional impassibility of God, it also opens up God (and our understanding of him) to all sorts of charges of inauthenticity and, indeed, immorality.

There are essentially three objections to any such glib answer to the problem. The first is that it raises what appear to me – and to many others – to be morally unanswerable objections to the perceived nature of God. For what kind of God is it who is himself impassible and yet 'allows' himself to suffer somewhat neatly and conveniently in the human person of Jesus? Even if Jesus is the Christ, and therefore the Second Person of the Trinity, there remains a metaphysically unbridgeable gulf between the human suffering of Jesus (even if within this one allows for suffering by the Second Person of the Trinity) and the notion of any suffering by an impassible God and therefore by the Trinity *in toto*. Human suffering becomes a vicarious substitute for any real notion of genuine divine suffering. And this fact leads directly to all of the dilemmas which surround so many concepts of the atonement: whether Jesus' suffering was sacrificial, expiatory, substitutionary or whatever, it still remains a 'let off' and a morally irresponsible and vicious requirement if God (as Father, as entire Trinity) is not held to suffer also.

The second objection is that this self-evident dichotomy within the Trinity – one Person who suffers, others who do not –

leads to an overwhelming perception of a schizophrenic God. It is hard (indeed even impossible) to imagine a father who does not suffer as his son suffers, and yet here is God pulling off the trick to perfection. This degree of moral absenteeism would be bad enough even in any human situation, yet here the Father and the Son are even supposed to be one! But what kind of oneness is it when the Father can watch the Son suffering without being moved or changed by it? It suggests not a God of one nature but of two quite distinct and opposing personalities, which is hardly what orthodox Christianity has otherwise attempted to proclaim!

The third objection is perhaps even more pressing and cogent than the first two, as it derives not from contemporary thought or speculation about the nature of God but from the record of scripture itself. Thus the doctrine of God's impassibility is not, finally, consistent with the record of scripture, especially (but not exclusively) that of the Old Testament. The God who appears in the Old Testament is anything but impassible, and indeed, compared with the God who positively leaps out of the pages of the Hebrew scriptures, the impassible God of patristic metaphysical perfection seems like an etiolated and feeble shadow of his former self. In the Old Testament God is vitally and passionately engaged with his people. He is tender, angry, loving, vengeful, and not averse to abrupt (and sometimes apparently irrational) changes of heart. It would be tedious in the extreme to quarry the Old Testament for each and every example of God's changeability, but the essence of this perception of God appears in many of the prophets and perhaps especially in Hosea. It is hard to reconcile a passage such as the following with any sense of divine impassibility:

> Will they not return to Egypt and will not Assyria rule over them because they refuse to repent? Swords will flash in their cities, will destroy the bars of their gates, and put an end to their plans. My people are determined to turn from me. Even if they call to the Most High, he will by no means exalt them. How can I give you up, Ephraim? How can I hand you over

Israel? How can I treat you like Admah? How can I make you like Zeboiim? My heart is changed within me; all my compassion is aroused. I will not carry out my fierce anger, nor will I turn and devastate Ephraim. For I am God and not man – the Holy One among you. I will not come in wrath.
(Hosea 11:5-9)

Furthermore, lest the charge be made – unjustified though it is – that the Old Testament is somehow 'subordinate' to the New Testament, it should be noted that exactly the same change of heart is reflected in, for example, Jesus' parable of the debtor servant. Indeed, here the change of heart is two-fold, from wrath to compassion and back to wrath again in the face of the servant's refusal to forgive his own debtor. Of course this is only a parable and we are not intended to push parallels too far and see the master as 'being' God, but at the same time Jesus surely devised his stories as windows onto aspects of God as well as into human behaviour.

Classical metaphysics, then, presents us with a major problem in attempting to do anything like justice to the nature and activity of God. It is a natural attribute of the human mind to wish to order and classify things, but as applied to God the theoretical perfections of metaphysics are just too restricting. Metaphysical thought is capable of perfect tidiness and, at the same time, and not entirely coincidentally, sterility: God appears to be rather less tidy but rather more dynamic than the categories of metaphysics readily allow for.

The only way forward, therefore, seems to be to re-open the gap – which as we have commented earlier has been all too often ignored – between metaphysics and the reality which it purports to describe. We must acknowledge that all of our speech about God – even apparently precise metaphysical speech – is only in the nature of the most halting picture or metaphor. What this means in practical theological terms is that whilst it may be true that God cannot logically create a square circle, nonetheless there may be present within God qualities which seem to us, with our limitations of perception, to be inconsistent – for what is inconsistent in time may turn out, without illogicality, to be entirely consistent within eternity. We need to avoid first applying human metaphysical terms to notions about God and then applying them to him, but instead learn to turn the spectacles around and ask first what seems from our experience, prayer and so on to be the nature of God, and then ask what terms we can find to describe, however inadequately (and in the full knowledge that any description will be inadequate) this nature.

Thus experientially – and also very importantly within the record of scripture – we appear to have to do with a God who is anything but impassible, is indeed, rather, a passionate God. Passion is not a term which we perhaps often associate with God, and yet as we shall see in Chapters Six and Seven particularly, there is a much neglected place for passion not only within our understanding of the life of God but within the human theological and spiritual realm also. The positing of such a passionate nature, though, is the only thing which makes sense of the scriptural witness to both the tenderness of God and the wrath of God. It also solves at least some of the ethical problems surrounding the crucifixion and brings a more moral dimension into the 'transactions' involved in the cross if we can begin to speak of God suffering – really suffering – as Father and as Holy Spirit in the crucifixion and not merely suffering vicariously through the human flesh of Jesus whilst leaving the Godhead impassibly unaffected by earthly events.

The question, then, is how can this perception of God be reconciled with the valuable insight which the doctrine of impassibility was attempting to convey, namely that God is not fickle or inconsistent, but constant and unchanging? In fact, the resolution of this question is not insolubly difficult once the metaphysical shackles of total impassibility have been broken. From the idea of impassibility we can draw the idea of God's constancy and eternity, and from the sources outlined above we can posit the concept of a passionate God who is capable of change. What emerges is a picture of a God who is unchanging in nature and purpose and who has a settled will for good and a settled nature of love, but who also has the capacity to feel moved to different responses and actions by human good or evil. Thus God's essence may be unchanging, but God is 'changeable' in his passionate nature.

This conception of God is a far cry from that which has too often held sway over Christian theology and ethics, and this setting free of God from the absolute claims of metaphysical description enables us to explore many new and creative avenues, both for our spirituality and for our ethical decision making. First, however, we must consider further the ways in which – freed from the exclusive use of Latin and Greek metaphysical categories – we may today most fruitfully envisage and describe the nature of God. That, at least, is the purpose of the succeeding chapter.

CHAPTER THREE

Pictures not a Definition

We have argued in the previous chapter that there is a pressing need for discovering new ways of speaking about God. There our exploration of this need was primarily metaphysical, stemming from the fact that metaphysics causes insoluble problems for our understanding of God if it is pursued too exclusively and too restrictively. But there are other reasons also for this need, and it is the purpose of this chapter to explore some of them at least in outline.

Alongside the exclusiveness and restrictiveness of a purely metaphysical approach, then, there exists a primarily spiritual and ethical need to re-envision our ways of speaking about God. This stems from the fact that the traditional descriptions and definitions of God, while they may be helpful to some, may also, as was briefly alluded to earlier, serve actively to marginalise or cause acute pain to others – the example taken earlier being that of the potentially alienating influence of any absolute and inflexible insistence that God be addressed as 'Father'.

There is thus a two-fold need to act – both metaphysical and ethical/pastoral, and both of these were felicitiously expressed in a *Church Times* article in late 2003 by Jane Shaw, at present Dean of Divinity, Chaplain and Fellow of New College, Oxford. Her highlighting of the issues in this way also lends credence to the idea that the objections and problems which have been highlighted here with regard to the usual traditional expressions of faith and doctrine are not merely academic, but powerfully practical and pastoral as well. She writes:

What the churches fail to present publicly is a sense of the mystery and, ultimately, unknowability of God, and the humility that goes with that. There is a tradition within Christianity that suggests that God is so beyond our human understanding that we cannot ever know him, and it is only by acknowledging this that we can approach a glimpse of him.

This *via negativa*, or negative way, has thrived on the margins of the church in the mystics, from Dionysius the Areopagite to the author of *The Cloud of Unknowing* and St John of the Cross. They teach us that acknowledging the mystery of God takes us beyond our narrow, inadequate, all-too-human frames of reference for the divine.

But the churches have too often tended to domesticate God, laying claim to a certain knowledge of who God is, who God likes and what God wants. This leaves out the mystery – the transcendent God witnessed by a few disciples in the great moment of the transfiguration; that sense of the divine we glimpse in the paintings, music and writings of great artists.

It also leads to exclusion and condemnation rather than welcome and humility, when encountering different human beings.

It is almost uncanny to find someone of whom I have never previously heard writing, five hundred miles away and in an entirely different intellectual and cultural climate, almost exactly the same things which I have been expressing in sermons, seminars, lectures, articles, and most recently, here. Both in Oxford and in the rural west of Ireland, and, I suspect, in many other places also, it is time for a re-think. But how?

The first step is to take to heart the absolute provisionality – which both Jane Shaw and the previous chapter of this study attempt to do – of everything which is, has been, will be, or ever could be said about God. This applies across the board in every conceivable circumstance in which God is mentioned – academic lectures and treatises, synod debates, parish sermons and bible studies. I have commented previously (in the context of toleration versus celebration) on just how far the church needs to travel if real progress is to be made, and this issue perhaps even more than that one is a case in point.

The movement towards this complete and humble admission of provisionality has been most noticeable at the level of academic study. Much has been said and written about metaphor, imagery and symbol, about the mystery of God, and the *via negativa* is once again a respectable theological way. Yet even within academia, however, there is still a plethora of voices (often conflicting) which argue for the absolute rightness of their views – God is this or that or does or does not do such and such. And ironically this applies as much to post-modernist and deconstructionist theologians as it does to, for example, conservative evangelical ones: the latter may be convinced that God only approves of certain moral actions, but the former are equally sure that God is only what we have created him to be, and neither account smacks of the necessary provisionality.

If there is still progress to be made at the academic level, then there is a huge abyss of unwillingness, fear, prejudice and sheer terror at the loss of familiarity to be bridged at the level of ordinary church members, whether in parishes or even in the governing bodies and councils of national church life. A single example will serve to illustrate this with lightning-like clarity. A few years ago the Church of Ireland produced a major report on sectarianism, and I was commissioned to write the theological preface to the report, exploring both the theology which underpins sectarianism and the sort of theological approaches which must be followed if we are to undo sectarianism and move away from it. In essence, the thesis of this preface was similar (although in a different context) to that advanced here. I argued that sectarianism is, effectively, a form of idolatry in which things of the second order (identity, culture, denomination, history and so on) are reified and allowed to take precedence over things of the first order of importance. Furthermore, in this process, God is defined in such a way as to meet the requirements of the group concerned, such that they can be convinced that he is 'on their side' and that, conversely, they can remain invincibly assured that their position or cause is therefore right. The counterbalance to this was, I suggested, the mystery of God and the possibility that in any of our definitions or explanations of God we may be entirely wrong, and that therefore the way out of sectarianism is, in part at least, finding the humility to acknowledge the provisionality of everything in our religious and theological life, even when this touches our most deeply held convictions or impinges on our own individual or group identity.

The response to this report – and in particular to the theological preface – was eye-opening. A very few speakers made commendatory remarks, but a far greater number objected to the lack of hard-line definitions, and one speaker even said – which with a beautiful irony proved most perfectly the whole point which the preface was trying to make – 'We need to know the certainties'!

And the whole point, which must be made again and again and again, is that there are no certainties! This is not either defeatist or agnostic – and certainly not atheistic – but merely realistic. I am as committed as anyone to my Christian faith and to my convictions about God, but behind all of these there stands the stark realisation that I may be wrong.

This realisation is vital, for the presence or absence of such a realisation will finally govern what we think we are doing when we do theology. Without it we are in danger of assuming a one-to-one correspondence between our thought and language and God himself; with it, we acknowledge that all of our God-talk is in the nature of picture, metaphor, symbol, model and so on. Not only may it be wrong, but it is provisional in the sense that it is not eternally unchangeable. This is a perspective which is reinforced by the best of modern philosophical as well as theological thinking, and is represented by, for example, Iris Murdoch's idea of 'disposable metaphor' which appears throughout her philosophical oeuvre. Pictures and metaphors can be employed for as long as they are genuinely useful, and may then quite properly be discarded, and even if one picture remains useful this does not stop us from generating others alongside it which may complement it or correct some deficit or allow a different perception to emerge.

Thus the recognition of provisionality allows us completely to re-define and creatively re-evaluate our relationship with the riches of the Christian tradition which we have inherited. Previously it has been assumed that this inheritance – because it has been supposed to communicate God in some 'once for all' sense – is non-negotiable: this and this only is Christianity. The faith must be expressed in these terms and mean precisely these things, and as far as anyone who tries to uncross a 't' or undot an 'i' is concerned, then, in the words of the so-called Athanasian Creed, 'Let them be anathema'. The effect of this rigidity of attitude is to exclude people from the church either by expelling them or by making them feel unable to enter in the first place, an experience which was emphatically that even of such an earnest spiritual seeker as Simone Weil who wrote:

> ... there is an absolutely insurmountable obstacle to the incarnation of Christianity. It is the use of the two little words *anathema sit*. I remain with all those things that cannot enter the church, the universal repository, because of those two little words.
>
> (*Simone Weil: An Anthology*, Ed. Sian Miles, London, Virago Press, 1986, p.41)

A thoroughgoing and radical – and consistently applied – doctrine of provisionality (equivalent to a contemporary re-discovery of the *via negativa*) significantly changes all of this, however. What we have inherited is not a blueprint of God himself. Certainly it is a record of human experience and interpretation of God and his activity, but this is, crucially, not quite the same thing. Our legacy, largely, is creeds, doctrinal statements, forms of worship, and indeed an entire religious worldview which is almost exclusively couched in the language of Greek and Latin philosophy and metaphysics. This is entirely consistent with the development of our faith, and there is nothing intrinsically wrong with this. Our faith was first given expression in an age when these were the common linguistic and epistemological coinage, and many of the greatest minds over a period of several hundred years have fashioned expressions of the faith which

have sustained and nurtured and inspired Christians for generation after generation. But, importantly, this achievement is not
the same thing as 'identifying' or 'capturing' God, and for all the
greatness of the achievement, the wisdom of these centuries
should not be reified and turned into the reality of God himself.
Provisionality dictates that even these classic formulations are
themselves provisional. Vital and foundational they may have
been to Christianity, but they are still nothing more than a series
of pictures, metaphors and symbols which stand to be interpreted
alongside, and even on occasions amended or corrected by,
those of succeeding generations.

Furthermore, we need to find the scope to allow individuals
to respond freely to the pictures produced across the theological
ages. Thus even today there are undoubtedly many people for
whom the formulations of previous generations remain entirely
meaningful, and their response to these pictures must continue
to be upheld as valid. At the same time, though, there will be
those for whom these 'classical' pictures have become drained of
meaning and may even be alienating, and for them – given the
primacy of provisionality – there must be allowed the freedom
to attempt, at least, to forge new metaphors which speak with
renewed vigour of their experience of God. The rich gallery of
images which we have inherited needs to be balanced by a
plethora of new and creative images of God – some of which will
last and others of which, like many from previous generations,
will eventually be found to be of limited use and will then sink
from view.

It would be unfair to suggest that this process has not at least
been begun, thanks to the strenuous efforts of theologians in a
variety of branches of the subject. Three very different examples
spring immediately to mind. The first is that which is known as
'feminist theology'. In fact the diversity of issues addressed and
the breadth of opinions held by those who would identify themselves by this or some such similar label is so vast and so valuable that it seems almost unfair to lump them together in this
way as though all are saying the same things. There is, however,

one connecting thread which, whatever the diversities, does seem to allow for a sense of collective identity, and that is a powerful and long overdue reaction against the church's masculine and patriarchal understanding both of its own internal organisation and, indeed, of God. Thus women (and men) have protested against the male-oriented and dominated structures, hierarchy, procedures and ways of thinking of the church and, even more significantly, they have reacted against the church's hijacking of male gender to describe God. Remarks have been made earlier in this study about the unhelpfulness to some (perhaps many) people of our traditional insistence on God as 'Father', but this is only one of several reasons why the feminist theologians have striven so hard to re-fashion our thinking about God. Most especially, perhaps, there has been a sense that just as the church lost out for far too long because it refused to countenance the idea of women in the ordained ministry, so too it has been almost wilfully impoverishing its spiritual resources by its refusal to pay serious attention to the concept of the feminine and maternal aspects of God. Yes, there may have been a willingness to open a back door to such ideas through concepts such as the feminine personification of Wisdom (*Sophia*), but this only scratches the surface of the issue since Wisdom, however significant, is only ever the 'handmaid' of God and never an ontological part of deity itself.

The feminist movement in theology, then, has done two things. First, it has fruitfully quarried the past and discovered – or re-discovered – that God has been envisaged in metaphors of femininity and maternity in previous generations, even if these have been downplayed or even largely ignored. The classic example of this in the English language would be the work of Julian of Norwich, although there are many more (and especially among the medieval and mystical) writers who are not afraid of the feminine attributes of God.

Secondly, and even more importantly, the feminist theology movement has brought these medieval insights into the present, and argued cogently and often passionately for the riches which a re-integration of femininity and maternity would bring to our understanding of, and relationship to divinity. Yes, 'Father' remains a valid concept, but so too does 'Mother' – as life-giver, nurturer, encourager and so on, and also as the validation of what it means to be feminine: men can no longer claim any sense of superiority – indeed it was ludicrous ever to do so – for God, in so far as gender applies at all when speaking of divinity, is at least as much feminine as masculine. Neither sex is privileged either ontologically or practically over the other: both are privileged in that both resemble at least some of the essential qualities and attributes of God.

If feminist theology as a movement has helped us – and sometimes battered us – to re-envision God in terms of gender, then my second example concerns a single theologian who has encouraged us to re-visit tradition and set free the passionate God (regardless of gender) who has, for too long been imprisoned there. This theologian is Jürgen Moltmann, and out of all of the varied contributions he has made to modern theology, the one which is germane here is his identification of God as a suffering and therefore – as we have argued earlier – a passible God. Here again is a new image, and one in which, powerfully and passionately, the suffering of the human Jesus is allowed to impinge upon the eternal heart and reality of God. Once the connection between human and divine suffering is thus made, the way is open for further fruitful reflection upon the relationship not only between Jesus and God, but between the whole of humanity and God, and the interaction between God and his world becomes once again a dramatic and creative theological and spiritual interface.

My third example, unlike the previous two, is not drawn from what might be called the 'professional' Christian realm of theologians or priests, and it is all the more significant for that, since it suggests that the awareness of the importance of the task of creating new metaphors and symbols of God is not restricted to this 'professional' class, but is, whether consciously reflected upon or not, a living and stimulating component in the faith of 'ordinary' – if that is not too insulting a term – Christians. This is the fact that it has frequently been artists and sculptors and writers who have either encouraged or challenged us to see God in new ways. Admittedly there has always been a large amount of relatively unquestioning and 'traditional' art alongside this, but a significant minority of creative artists have asked us to respond to their work by thinking again about how we understand both God him/herself and our relationship to him/her.

Often this has been done through new interpretations of the person of Jesus Christ. I think immediately of two examples from entirely different media – the production of a variety of sculptures portraying a black Jesus, and the film (in spite of the hackles it raised at the time) based on Nikos Kazantzakis' book, *The Last Temptation of Christ*. Each of these interpretations has offered a fresh perspective and invited us to see anew some aspect of the person of Christ.

To begin with the black Christs. No, of course Jesus was not literally black – but, being a middle easterner, neither was he creamy-white as so much of art would suggest! The purpose of the sculptures is not to make literal claims about Jesus, but to convey visually the reality that as the Christ he is for all, regardless of race or colour. It is a way of 'owning' Christ for other cultures than the white western one, and it is a reminder to that white western culture that Jesus Christ is not our 'possession'. He was and is the Christ for all. As a symbolic representation of the universality of Jesus Christ this is religious art at its creative and perspective-broadening best.

Doubtless even a black Christ is a little much for some people, but an image such as this is placed in the shade when viewed alongside the film *The Last Temptation of Christ*. This attracted charges of blasphemy and was found by many people to be grossly offensive. I suggest, however, that this was a knee-jerk traditionalist and conservative reaction to something which upset a great many pre-conceptions about Jesus, and that the 'message' of the film was consequently not even assimilated by most of its critics. At any rate it deserves close attention here.

The film was accused of blasphemy because of one particular scene in which Jesus, whilst on the cross, is tempted by the possibility of an alternative to death – as divine he could escape the cross and live with Mary Magdalene – and there follows a visualisation of this life including sexual intercourse. What most of the film's critics forgot to mention, though, is that the end of the film shows this temptation being vigorously rejected, and Jesus from the cross once again accepting the cross and his imminent death.

So what is the film doing? Visually and grippingly, I suggest, it is reminding us of the absolute full humanity of Jesus. So often, whether in the gospels (especially St John's gospel) and even more in art, we are presented with an almost docetic Christ to whom suffering (and also, incidentally, temptation) seem almost immaterial. The cross is turned into high art, and the smell of fear and dirt, the embarrassment of nakedness and the brutality of soldiers and crowd are all but forgotten as a serene Christ dies gracefully. *The Last Temptation* shocks by utterly destroying this calm 'religious' aura of the cross, and showing us both the cruelty of the death and the total humanity of Jesus – yes, he did have a very real sexuality says the film. Moulds are broken, idols shattered perhaps – and yet the end is orthodox as Jesus dies on the cross: what is different is that we have seen – perhaps even unwillingly – something more of the cost and the reality of this death and have discovered that Jesus was in his humanity exactly like us. Blasphemous, no: challenging and paradigm-shifting, yes, and to that extent again genuinely religious art.

All of the above examples are valid attempts to expand the range of our references and responses to God, and to provide new pictures and images through which different facets of God and the divine activity may be communicated. All of them, however, and as far as I am aware, the vast majority of similar efforts, concentrate on one or another aspect of God and do not address themselves to the fullness of Trinitarian life. Certainly, as I trust has been demonstrated by these examples, it is important to explore any and every aspect of God in new ways, but it is equally important to explore the totality of God as Trinity in new ways also.

There may be any number of reasons for this need, including the need to find alternatives to 'Father' for those for whom this term is not helpful, but there is one which seems to me to be of especial significance. Again it should be stressed that in advancing an alternative model I am not advocating abandoning the terms Father, Son and Holy Spirit. These remain and still convey their own profound meaning which many of us – myself included – still find evocative and rich both theologically and in prayer. I am merely suggesting that Father, Son and Holy Spirit is not the only way in which we may express the life of God, and by the canons of provisionality we are quite entitled to supply another picture or pictures to complement this one. My principal reason, then, for wanting to set another Trinitarian model alongside the traditional one is concerned with attempting to balance the immanence of God with his transcendence. The terms Father, Son and Holy Spirit of course speak of both immanence and transcendence, but the 'weight' of the model is more transcendent than immanent in spite of the Incarnation. God is the glorious creator, the (now) risen and ascended Son, and the Holy Spirit who may be immanent but is also so mysterious as to be powerfully 'other' and transcendent. And furthermore, also adding to this weight of transcendence, this particular set of relationships – a Father, a metaphysically 'begotten' Son, and a Spirit who may be identifiable with either or both or neither of these at certain times – is one which is unique to God: we have no relational hold on it or intuitive understanding of what these relationships might be like. For all of St Patrick's putative shamrock illustration or the well-worn ice, water and steam model, this set of relationships is not reflected or even recognisable anywhere else except in God.

Thus I suggest that we need a parallel understanding of the Trinity which speaks of immanence with more weight, and which employs relationships which we do instinctively understand and share. Again, another brief disclaimer: I am not denying the uniqueness of God; by definition God is unique however we choose to describe him/her. But at the same time this unique

God, however mysterious and ineffable, needs to be envisioned, however imperfectly and inadequately, in ways which resonate with our own human understandings and feelings if we are to experience the fullness of a relationship with him/her. For some the model of Father, Son and Holy Spirit may be entirely adequate for the purpose: for others it may, as we have suggested, be inadequate or even off-putting, and for such people other models (which are equally only pictures as, however hallowed it may be, the model of Father, Son and Holy Spirit is also) may prove helpful. A complementary picture will be no more a definition of God than Father, Son and Holy Spirit actually is; but it may enable us to find another window – in this case one which is rooted in our own embodied state – into the boundless riches, fullness and love which we believe constitutes the heart of God.

So then, I wish to propose just one picture (and others may well wish to contribute further pictures) to set alongside the traditional one of Father, Son and Holy Spirit, and my intention and hope is that it is a picture which may enable us to find connections between our own embodied state (and therefore our embodied loving) and God him/herself, such that God comes to be experienced as a more meaningful part of our human loving, and our love for God becomes itself strengthened by that human and embodied experience of loving.

I should, of course, add that the model I wish to propose is essentially a rediscovery of a model that is the best part of 1500 years old, and which stems from the thinking of St Augustine of Hippo. The terms used, therefore, are his but their precise interpretation and use are mine. In this form the model first saw the light of day – as did the central ideas for this book – at the 2003 Glenstal Ecumenical Conference. Furthermore its reception there among both heterosexuals and homosexuals, men and women, was enthusiastic. The model, then, is essentially very simple and firmly Trinitarian in shape: simply that we conceive of the persons of the Trinity as The Lover, The Beloved and The Love which flows between them.

The strength of this model is, I suggest, both its radical difference in terminology from the traditional formulation, and yet its substantial consonance with it in terms of the properties which may be ascribed by it to each person of the Trinity. Thus, in the terminology involved there is both an avoidance of any resemblance to the potentially off-putting nature of the traditional terms, and also there is opened up to us a wide new range of relational possibilities and images through the use of this model.

Equally importantly, though, in terms of remaining within the limits of permissible (if sometimes radical) orthodoxy, many of the relational insights generated by the model of Father, Son and Holy Spirit are retained here, as is the essential traditional Trinitarian structure of the Christian faith.

First, the primacy of the First Person of the Trinity is preserved: the one who loves is prior (in an ontological, even if not a temporal sense) to all that is loved, and incidentally the notion (present but often underplayed in Christianity) of the creation of everything in and through the power of that love is thereby enhanced.

Secondly, it remains pictorially true to suggest that the Beloved is in a very real sense 'begotten' by the love of the Lover – for it is only this which creates or bestows the status of the Beloved. Similarly also it can be argued (rather as St Paul argues for a 'retrospective' designation of Sonship through resurrection in the first chapter of Romans) that the Beloved comes to fullness and vindication of that status by his unconditional returning of the Lover's begetting love.

Thirdly, as with any lover and beloved, the love which flows between them is at once independent of each (being in fact the creation of both and therefore identical with neither of them but rather a separate entity on its own) and yet intimately connected with each – and indeed being of the essence of each – much as the Holy Spirit is traditionally conceived of as being.

In principle, then, there is both much that is new – in terms of possibilities – and much that is consonant with orthodoxy and tradition in this model of the Trinity of love. In order further to explore the nature of God's love, and indeed also the nature of our own human love which this model points to, the next step is to pause and to consider what forms of love exist and which of these is capable of conveying or imaging divinity. Is the traditional primacy of *agape* really as unassailable as Christianity has most often traditionally assumed?

CHAPTER FOUR

Eros and Agape

Love is almost certainly the most overworked and abused word in the English language. It is used to cover what is in fact a multitude of emotions, some deep and powerful, some transient, fickle and even superficial. 'I love you'; 'I love my country'; 'I love Mozart'; 'I love sausage and chips'. The verb employed is the same in each case, but the underlying meaning (and force and gravity) is entirely different.

It is indeed hardly surprising that this profusion (and confusion) of meaning should exist, since the one word 'love' in English does duty for at least four separate Graeco/Latin terms which define much more closely the various qualities and characteristics of different kinds of love.

The wide variety of meanings conveyed by the word 'love' was perhaps most famously delineated by C. S. Lewis in his celebrated book *The Four Loves*, which appeared as long ago as 1960. Very briefly, then, to summarise his work: Lewis identified four types of love, entitled affection, friendship, eros and charity. Each of these has different characteristics and objects, and each has an assigned place in a scale of values. For Lewis the highest of them is charity, which is the kind of love, Lewis argues, which God bestows on his creation and, as divine, is therefore the kind of love to which we should aspire. It is a 'gift-love' and not a 'need-love', and it is directed primarily towards the well-being of its object.

Lewis uses his own terms to describe his four loves, but what he chooses to call charity has a great deal in common with what the bulk of the Christian tradition has often chosen to call *agape*, and it is significant that whichever name is used, *agape* or charity has always been envisioned as being both entirely distinct from and qualitatively superior to *eros*. It is instructive to establish a little more fully just how this ecclesiastical value-judgement on love originated and why it has proved so psychologically deep-rooted and temporally enduring.

It is probably fair to say that this 'ordering' of loves stems largely from the early Church Fathers rather than from scripture itself, and certainly not from the Jewish heritage of Christianity, for Judaism has always had – and certainly so in its scriptures – a much more earthy and passionate appreciation of the nature of God than Christianity itself has often done.

The birthplace of this idea of a hierarchy of loves was almost certainly the prevailing Graeco-Latin philosophical culture in which Christianity grew up. Both Stoicism and Platonism, for example, although in many respects very different, shared common assumptions about the superiority of the spiritual over the physical, the disembodied over the embodied: and Christianity, it appears, simply baptised this complex of ideas and adapted it for its own use.

That this should have happened at all is somewhat surprising, for one might imagine that an Incarnational faith would have a certain amount of time for physicality and embodiedness! One might have expected a radical re-evaluation of the physical dimension of existence, but this never materialised. Instead the new faith took on the philosophical values of its time, and indeed, over succeeding generations intensified the division between spirit and matter, soul and body, driving a wedge between spirituality and sexuality which has been with us ever since.

We have already mentioned the Desert Fathers in a previous chapter, but we must re-visit their influence here also. There is no doubting the purity and even the validity of their intentions, for initially at least they were concerned primarily to remove themselves from the thrall of daily business and social living in order to devote themselves more fully to contemplation and the spiritual life. However, at a very early stage this intention was

compromised by an almost competitive asceticism in which individuals strove to 'subdue' or 'repress' the flesh in ever more
extreme and long-lasting ways, whether by fasting, sleep depri-
vation or actual physical self-punishment.

The result was, largely, that what began as an exercise in soli-
tary contemplation and prayer rapidly turned into something
else: a holy war against the flesh which now came to be seen as
necessarily sinful and which should be escaped from or sub-
dued as much as possible. Spirituality had become divorced
from physicality, and the foundations of a two thousand year religious schizophrenia between soul and body, spirit and matter,
had been laid down.

This legacy of the Desert Fathers was then further explored,
rationalised, theologised and woven into the fabric of church
life, doctrine and devotion over the succeeding three centuries
or so. One might trace its growth through a wide variety of figures, but it is sufficient here to isolate two of them: one of whom
exemplifies the destructive potential born of a growing fear of
embodiment, and the other one of whom both exhibits in his
own character and actions a move from a powerful sense of erotic
love to what might best be described as a 'spiritual lovelessness',
and who also, through his thought and writing, has destructively
governed the mind-set of the Christian Church towards sexuality
and embodiment – at least in its official attitudes – ever since.

The first of these figures is the second and third century theologian, biblical commentator and writer on spirituality, Origen,
who lived from about 185-254 AD. In view of our previous remarks about Christianity and its baptism of Stoic and Platonic
philosophical ideas, it is interesting that Origen is one of the
Christian thinkers most deeply influenced by the Stoicised
Middle-Platonism which prevailed in the Hellenistic culture of
his time. For Origen the world is a pale (and inferior) reflection
of the true spiritual world, and as Benjamin Drewery points out
in the 1983 edition of *A Dictionary of Christian Spirituality*, there
are in Origen's thought, 'echoes of the Platonic "wherefore we
ought to fly away from earth to heaven as quickly as we can".'

Indeed, the world should be left behind as quickly as possible, and preferably by martyrdom (cf his treatise *Exhortation to Martyrdom*), which is, I suppose, the ultimate mortification of the flesh!

Origen was undoubtedly possessed of one of the finest minds of his time, and his thought and writing profoundly influenced the church both in his own lifetime and afterwards, but behind the warp of all of his creative thinking lay a dark and negative weft of fear: fear of embodiment in general and of sexuality in particular. The body existed only in order to be resisted, especially in the realm of sexuality, and indeed it is said that Origen was so afraid of the compulsive power of sexuality that he castrated himself – this being the only way to ensure ultimate 'victory' over his own sexual urges and temptations. Origen may be unique among Christian theologians in having taken such a drastic step, but many other individuals (and the church community and hierarchy in general) have shared his deep-seated fear of, and negative attitude towards embodiment and sexuality.

Origen's fears resulted in dramatic consequences for himself, but the other figure I propose to examine briefly succeeded in encumbering the entire human race with the consequences of his fears. This figure is St Augustine of Hippo whom we have briefly encountered in the previous chapter as the begetter of the alternative Trinitarian model of the Lover, the Beloved and the Love which flows between them. Notwithstanding this remarkable and positive contribution, however, Augustine was (and is) also responsible for some of the most negative and destructive trends in Christian thinking, especially in the realm of sexuality.

Augustine, as he appears in his own *Confessions*, was a hugely complex character. He was also a profound and powerful thinker and a man capable of intense passion, and he is central to our argument here, both for the way in which his mistrust of sexuality affected his own thought, and for the immense influence which his thought has had on theology and church life ever since.

By his own account Augustine, in his early life, was a man

who not only accepted but indeed rejoiced in his own sexuality, keeping a concubine and indeed having a son by her. On his conversion to Christianity, however, all of this changed – to borrow some words of Yeats', 'changed utterly' – such that 'a terrible beauty was born'. For beauty there undoubtedly was in Augustine's Christian life and thought: the best of his writing, whether theological, confessional or devotional, has a wonderful clarity and breathes with a sense of both the immanence and mystery of God.

But the beauty was terrible nonetheless, both in terms of its effect upon Augustine and in terms of his enduring theological legacy, for in embracing Christianity Augustine rejected sexuality. The reasons for doing this were undoubtedly complex ones, and, in part, virtuous ones, in terms of wanting to leave behind what he now saw as the immoral (and indeed damnable) libertinism of his past life, but the problem was (and is) that Augustine did not merely leave behind his own past but also condemned it and then, from the deep well of his own guilt, made the fatal association of sexuality in all its forms with innate sinfulness.

The supreme expression of this is, of course, his exposition of – and indeed one might almost say obsession with – the idea of original sin. This doctrine as expounded by Augustine and by much of the church after him, has two profoundly negative consequences. First, original sin is passed on by the act of procreation, and thus every sexual act – even the most supposedly moral one of intercourse between husband and wife – is tainted with sin, in the sense that even if not actually sinful in itself it is nonetheless the means by which humanity's innate sinfulness (and guilt) is passed on. Secondly, it means that we are each burdened with sin from the moment of birth – we are sinful simply by virtue of being live embodied beings. The idea of the body as something impure and to be escaped from is thereby powerfully reinforced, and Christians are condemned to go through life not only as exiles from the heavenly city but also, in a metaphorical sense, as prisoners in their own bodies and at the same time as exiles from any real intuition as to how to live fulfilled lives within those bodies. Such has been the uncomfortable schizophrenic relationship with their own bodies which Christians have struggled to live with ever since. No wonder that the church is still in such a muddled mess about bodies and the whole notion of embodiment even today!

Furthermore, alongside this downplaying and denigrating of the manifestations of sexuality, there ran a parallel current which removed all talk of genuine 'love' onto another plane entirely. Physical expressions of love were at worst mere lust and at best a very second rate *erotic* form of love, not to be compared to the higher loves of *caritas* or *agape*, which related more nearly – it was supposed – to the divine love. Divine love was one thing: human love – unless subsumed into the divine *agape* – was quite another thing, and, by definition, immeasurably inferior to it.

Such, at least, has been the 'mainstream' Christian approach to sexuality, and certainly the one which has, throughout the ages, underpinned the church's official pronouncements on sexuality. Sexuality has been seen as a powerful, but largely dark, motivating force, which needs to be channelled into the one appropriate setting, that of marriage, where, even if it cannot exactly be celebrated, it can at least be tolerated.

Thankfully, however, this has never been the only – although it has always been the predominant – Christian voice as far as sexuality is concerned. For there has always been a more holistic and wholesome – though in the official eyes of the church also subversive – voice on sexuality running parallel to this mainstream one. This voice has indeed been one which has not only celebrated and rejoiced in the language of sexuality, but one which has also infiltrated this language into that of spirituality and prayer, thus offering an as yet largely untapped means by which the long-separated realms of body and soul may yet be reintegrated and placed in a more positive relationship one to the other.

This voice, of course, is that, for the most part, of the mystics, who have rediscovered an aspect of spirituality which has been long forced underground but which equally has a long history stretching back to such biblical writings as the *Song of Songs* and to the rich biblical imagery of God as husband, lover and so on. Here there is the language of passion and sexuality applied in all its richness and evocativeness to spirituality in order to describe the full depth of God's love for us and of our response to God. It is the language not merely of an intellectual assent or a love of the mind, or even of the heart, but of the whole person as we respond to God with every fibre of our being, both body and soul. Of course such language, when applied to God, is metaphorical, as is any language which attempts to encapsulate the love of God in human terms, but it is evocative language nonetheless which tries to express how thoroughgoing is God's love. That love is not some kind of divine academic exercise, but a love which emanates from the totality of God. And when it comes to our response to that love, the language ceases to be merely metaphorical and becomes a genuine reflection of the complex ways in which, at different times, we know ourselves to be moved to love in return: sometimes with a love from the head, sometimes from the heart, and sometimes with an overwhelming completeness which only the language of our most all-consuming human love (in other words, that which encompasses our sexuality) can even begin to do justice to.

There is no great merit in attempting to trawl through every mystic of every age by way of illustration. Rather, just two examples from the great age of European mysticism from the fourteenth to the sixteenth centuries will suffice. In the mid fourteenth century Richard Rolle could write:

How much more ought I to sing, and as sweetly as I can, to my Jesus Christ, my soul's spouse, through the whole of this present life. Compared with the coming brightness this life is 'night', and I too languish, and languishing, faint for love. But because I faint I shall recover, and be nourished by his warmth; and I shall rejoice, and in my joy sing jubilantly the delights of love ... my soul is ever avid to love; never through grief or sloth will she give up her accepted desire.

In even more explicit vein, St John of the Cross, writing around two hundred years later, has this to say in his *Songs of the Soul in Rapture:*

Oh night that was my guide!
Oh darkness dearer than the morning's pride,
Oh night that joined the lover
To the beloved bride
Transfiguring them each into the other.

and three stanzas later:

Lost to myself I stayed
My face upon my lover having laid
From all endeavour ceasing:
And all my cares releasing
Threw them amongst the lilies there to fade.

Here, and in many other similar passages, is the language of passion indeed.

The existence of this rich undercurrent and its relative obscurity begs the question of why has the church behaved thus with regard to sexuality? Why has this undercurrent always been mistrusted and either ignored or repressed by the 'official' voices of the church, and why, in just the same way, has *agape* always been valued above *eros* in the hierarchy of loves? Indeed, why has *eros* so often been seen not merely as a love inferior to *agape*, but as a love which should, whenever possible, be left behind or discarded in favour of *agape*?

The answer to this question is, I think, very simple, and rests upon the church's perception – going back not only to the Desert Fathers but right back into the mists of the origins of our Judaeo-Christian history – of one aspect of sexuality, and its consequent blindness (whether wilful or simply blinkered) to another aspect of it. The church, then, has long been aware of the sheer power of sexuality, and the recognition of this power has, throughout the whole of our Judaeo-Christian history, led to a culture of fear and taboo regarding all manifestations of sexuality and not merely those which are concerned with acts of genital sex. This fear emerges as early as the Jewish purity laws, according to which a menstruating woman is unclean, as is a woman after childbirth. This fear – which, admittedly may initially have had much to do with blood and primitive hygiene – is then radically intensified during the history of Christianity itself. Women in many ages come to be seen not merely as ritually unclean, but as quasi-demonic temptresses and as potential sources of evil to be avoided. Poor weak sinful men are so likely to be led astray by this wicked race that they are better to stay away from them entirely. Sex is seen as a powerful – indeed, all-consuming – force, which leads, almost inevitably, to sinful acts. It is the source of much evil and little, if any, good. Sexuality has been separated from spirituality because something so powerful must be kept in check by the church and not allowed to begin to impinge on – much less to influence – the higher realms of spirituality and *agape*.

What the church has rightly seen, then, is the power of sexuality. What it has equally been blind to, because it has seen in that power only the potential for destructiveness, is the equal potential within human sexuality for creativity and beauty. Such blindness to the creative potential of sexuality (and creative not merely or even primarily in the sense of procreative), and the concomitant obsession with the potential power for destructiveness in sexuality has influenced the church to view sexuality in all its forms (with the grudging exception of one specific act within heterosexual marriage) as intrinsically evil, and thus the whole realm of sexuality has found itself sitting in the 'bad' side of the moral scales.

Such a placing of sexuality on the side of the bad (and if you doubt it, recall again that the 1662 *Book of Common Prayer* gives one pressing, if grudging, reason for marriage as 'the avoidance of sin'), raises a whole series of further questions, first about the nature of embodiment and its desires, and our understanding of the God who created us this way; and secondly about where, in fact, morality ought to begin and in what qualities it should primarily be rooted.

Thus, in brief, it seems strange, indeed, not to say cruel, that

God should have created us with a body with such a wide range of potential feelings and expressions with regard to sexuality and then arbitrarily declared all but one of these feelings – and especially expressions – to be immoral. Even more pointedly, the blindness of the church referred to above raises the question of whether the concepts of 'good' and 'bad' – and who defines what is good or bad? – are even the right places to start as far as morality is concerned, or whether other criteria which may be more sensitive to a whole range of moral possibilities are not ultimately more suitable. These are issues which are merely noted here, but to which we will return in more depth in Chapter Five.

Here, in this chapter whose central focus is not right and wrong, but *eros* and *agape* and the church's understanding and ordering of human loves, it is, I simply suggest, time for the church to review its traditional and official positions in the light of the discovery of its own blindness to the rich creativity of sexuality, its ignoring or suppression of the erotic spirituality of a good deal of mystical writing, and the acknowledgement of its own fear of sexuality and indeed of embodiment which seem to run profoundly counter to what we might expect of a thorough-going religion of Incarnation.

We have, in a previous chapter, argued – at one level at least – for the possibility of God, and here we have argued equally that the church has misguidedly suppressed a strand in its own history and spirituality which has sought to relate that possibility to the human experience of loving, and which has unashamedly employed the language of *eros* to illuminate our embodied relationship with that possible God, who himself knew the fullness of embodiment in Jesus Christ.

What is needed now is for the church to begin fully to understand, and acknowledge, the passions of human love in the context of God and his love. If God is passible – in feeling, even if not in will – then this opens up the possibility of a truly passionate God; a God in respect of whom the metaphors, images and erotic resonances of the mystics are not inappropriate. Such a notion of God brings with it two major changes of emphasis and consequent benefits. First, it appears to be truer to the nature of

the God who is revealed in scripture – as we have previously argued – such that our own life of prayer and our relationship
with God may be seen to be more of a piece with its scriptural
roots and not divorced from it by the church's 'gloss' on this
God; and secondly it is truer to our understanding of ourselves
as embodied (and sexual) beings whose powerful feelings are
not necessarily intrinsically evil but are part and parcel of our
being made in the image of a passible and passionate God.

The freedom and potential which such an approach brings is
radical and far-reaching. Our embodied selves and our human
erotic loving are now no longer forced into spiritual subjugation
or relegated in the face of a supposedly higher *agape*, but are instead set free and potentially empowered as a means of experi-
encing and returning the passionate love which God has for us.
Our response to God is no longer confined to any supposed
higher love of head or heart, but is acknowledged to be a response which emanates from the whole of our embodied being,
and in which we can use the language and metaphor of sexuality,
poetry, imagination as well as the more formal language of liturgy
and doxology. And it may be argued that such a response is one
that is not only liberating but actually more true to the nature of
the God to whom we are responding. Thus, drawing on the rich
language of poetry, myth and imagination in the world of J. R. R.
Tolkein, Stratford Caldecott has the following to say about the
nature of the 'secret fire' in Tolkein's world:

> ... we might call it the divine *eros*. We normally associate
> God with love in the sense of *agape* or charity, and *eros* with
> the love of the sexes. But the word captures the passionate
> energy of God's love in a way that *agape* does not. The char-
> acteristic of *eros* is that it reaches out towards beauty: it is a
> response to beauty, or a recognition of it. In God's case it is
> the active creation of beauty. We find this wild, passionate,
> creative and fiery love of God enshrined in the very heart of
> the Bible as the *Song of Songs*.
> (*Secret Fire: The Spiritual Vision of J. R. R. Tolkein*, London,
> Darton, Longman and Todd, 2003, pp 107-8.)

Whatever we may personally make of Tolkein and the imaginative world which he created, this description seems to me to stand alone, regardless of Tolkein's 'secret fire', as a powerful evocation of the passionate nature of the God with whom we have to do and to whom we are called to relate with an equal passion using the medium of our whole selves and the whole spectrum of our human loving.

A vision of God and a freedom in relationship with him, such as we have outlined here, is full of creative potential, but its re-direction depends upon a number of factors. One of these, the dismantling of some of the weightier shackles of metaphysics has been discussed in an earlier chapter, but another equally substantial task is the re-envisioning of Christian ethics. Arguing that we should celebrate our sexuality and its place in spirituality in relationship with a passionate God is one thing: actually managing to do this in the face of traditional Christian ethics is quite another. And the major stumbling block is the sheer cruelty and inhumanity of much of this system of ethics, which is rooted in absolutes as supposedly final as God's equally supposed impassibility, and which consigns most of our sexuality to the realms of wickedness or damnation – or at least to the realm of confession and repentance. It is to the ironic task of undoing the immorality of Christian morality that we must now turn.

CHAPTER FIVE

The Cruelty of Christian Ethics

The central purpose of this book, as will have become clear by now, is to establish a new and more life-enhancing approach to ethics, but one which is nonetheless at home within an orthodox, if at times somewhat radically orthodox, understanding of Christianity. My contention is that doctrine and ethics are inextricably linked and that each exercises a profound influence upon the other. Thus what we believe about God will affect our understanding of right and wrong, and conversely our ideas about God will be shaped in part at least by the kinds of values and behaviours which we consider to be morally appropriate. The task is not an easy one, and it involves a continual process of crossing and re-crossing from doctrine to ethics and back again. We have already visited the territory of metaphysics and considered the passibility or impassibility of God, and now in this chapter it is important to make another link and to begin by exploring how and why this discussion of passibility or impassibility impinges so largely on any subsequent discussion of ethics.

Principally it does so because an ethics based on a metaphysically impassible God, whom we think we know or have some sort of handle on because he is unchanging and once known is therefore known for ever, has an inbuilt tendency to be equally impassible and unchanging. In the Judaeo-Christian tradition it has also, beginning with the Ten Commandments (which it is worth remembering were written on tablets of stone, and how's that for impassibility!), tended to be exclusivist, marginalising, guilt-inducing and largely negative in orientation. It is much easier to define what should not be done than it is to produce rules for what should be done, and the Ten Commandments reflect this, with eight of them beginning, 'Thou shalt not'. So firmly ingrained is this 'Thou shalt not' mentality in our tradition that even when we substitute for the Ten Commandments the two great commandments of love God and love your neighbour as yourself, there is still the deeply etched sub-text lurking at the back of our minds which says: 'And what this means is that thou shalt not do certain things'!

Thus one of the central problems of such a basis for ethics in an inflexible and impassible (and often negative) model of God is that it is itself inflexible and negative, and indeed is capable of immense cruelty and destruction. Undoubtedly this has been experienced by a very large number of individuals who have found themselves at variance with the church's teaching on one of several ethical issues, but it has equally in the past proved destructive to entire societies (such as certain parts of Polynesia) whose marital customs did not conform to those laid down by the inflexibly 'moral' Christian missionaries of the mid to late nineteenth century.

The other key problem with this kind of basis for ethics is that it also tends to boil down to some variety of 'because God says so' or 'because the bible says so' or a combination of the two. If this was ever in any real doubt, then two recent examples of precisely this attitude from very different parts of the Anglican Communion, although on the same subject, spring to mind. The first is part of the response of the 'Evangelical Fellowship of Irish Clergy' to a Bishops' Pastoral Letter on Human Sexuality. One sentence is sufficient to convey the flavour of this document, and its sentiments are repeated on numerous occasions within the space of only five or six A5 pages. The members of the Fellowship comment: 'We value the insights of Christian tradition and reason, provided they do not challenge the place of scripture as the final authority and ultimate court of appeal in matters of faith and lifestyle.' The second is from the Archbishop of Nigeria who has criticised recent events on the grounds of their 'unfaithfulness to scripture' which is a 'major life and death issue'.

All of this sounds wonderfully clear-cut and high-principled, but the issues are nowhere near as simple as this (widespread) position would try to make out, and the difficulties with attempting to maintain such a position with any sort of coherence or cogency are legion. Five such difficulties come immediately to mind.

The first – and we will deal with them in reverse order of importance, beginning with the most peripheral and working towards the centre of the problem – is that there are many contemporary moral issues on which the bible provides little or no guidance at all, simply because its authors had no idea that the situations involved might ever exist. Many areas of modern medical and biological ethics provide a prime example of this. Decisions must be made and some sort of ethical consensus reached, but the bible quite simply cannot function as a final court of appeal because it completely fails to address the issues involved. So, for example, whilst a traditionally-minded reader of the bible might be able to extrapolate ethical norms to govern embryo research on the grounds that 'thou shalt not kill', it is incredibly hard to see what the bible realistically has to say about the rights and wrongs of genetically modified crops or the use or cessation of use of a life-support machine.

Secondly, contrary to what the 'final authority' of scripture argument would have us believe, our use of scripture is already thoroughly subjective and selective. We have never stuck to it slavishly but interpreted it according to our best contemporary lights, and scripture sits under and not above that judgement. According to scripture it is wrong to wear garments of mixed materials; it is perfectly alright to own slaves (and even beat a slave to death providing that death occurs at least twenty-four hours after the beating); and we should, of course, be stoning adulterers. We have chosen to ignore the first of these commands as irrelevant, and feel the second and third to be themselves immoral. We have judged scripture and, in these and a myriad of other similar cases, found it wanting, or at least locked into its own ancient time and values and no longer rele-

vant or appropriate today. So even the most ardent 'final authority' advocate would be hard pressed not to concede, without
being either duplicitous or utterly disingenuous, that whatever
authority scripture (or parts of it) may have, this is an authority
which we ourselves have accorded to it, and not an innate authority simply because it is scripture. We are already selective,
and what is there to prevent us from extending that already
well-used principle of selectivity to other and newer issues, including that of human sexuality?

Thirdly, and very uncomfortably, the bible can sometimes be
self-contradictory, or at least not as clear as we might like it to
be. The 'final authority' argument would encourage us to regard
the bible as monolithic and uniform in its guidance – after all,
God's inspiration is there throughout and this cannot change.
What is forgotten, however, is that the bible is at least as much
about human interpretation and understanding of that inspiration as it is about the inspiration itself, and whilst God's inspiration may in theory be unchanging (although even this might
well be questioned, especially if God is passible), our human re-
ceptivity to and comprehension of it is certainly not unchanging.
Again, as with our selectivity towards the bible, any number of
examples could be cited, but for our purpose here (which is simply to establish the principle of biblical pluralism and potential
contradiction) one issue will suffice. A suitable, and often still
contentious one is the subject of divorce. Admittedly the
Anglican Church has in recent years relaxed its discipline and
agreed under certain circumstances, and at the discretion of the
clergyperson, to the re-marriage of divorced persons in church,
but the Roman Catholic Church is as adamant as ever on the in-
admissibility of divorce, and the position was (for the Anglican
Church) and is (for the Roman Catholic Church) largely underpinned by an appeal to scripture, in particular the prohibition on
divorce as a dominical saying in St Mark's gospel. However,
alongside this one saying there are at least two other New
Testament pronouncements on the subject, to say nothing of the
detailed procedures and grounds for divorce outlined in the

Books of the Law in the Old Testament. St Matthew, for example, softens St Mark's hard-line attitude by permitting divorce at least on the grounds of adultery, and in the epistles St Paul goes even further, appearing to countenance in 1 Corinthians the possibility of separation and even divorce on the grounds of the lack of faith of one's partner. Who is right and what is the 'biblical' stance on divorce? In the face of such contradictions the only option is to admit the plurality of voices and, as we have already discussed, exercise our judgement and be selective once more. Again, in its contradictions scripture stands under and not over against human judgement and selectivity.

These first three difficulties are ones which arise largely from within the text of scripture itself, but the fourth and fifth ones are more closely concerned with the ways in which we read scripture and employ it to justify our own particular positions. The fourth difficulty is in a sense the key one, for it is the one which fatally undoes the case for a straightforward and ultimate appeal to scripture. And this is vitally necessary, as otherwise it is all too easy for those who wish to make such an appeal to make others look faithless or sceptical or heretical. Thus the ultimate problem with the twin appeal to God and to scripture is that it is entirely circular and actually has no external validation whatsoever. It sounds impressive to say, 'God says so' or 'scripture says so', but that is all such an appeal amounts to: sound – mere rhetoric with no foundation outside itself. It is, in fact circular in two ways – one in general terms and one in specifically ethical terms.

Let me try to spell it out. First the general circularity of the argument. How do we know that God said such and such? Because it is in the scriptures. How do we know that the scriptures are authoritative? Because God says that they are. How do we know that God says that they are? Because it says so in the scriptures. How do we know that the scriptures are authoritative? And so on and so on and so on!

Secondly, the specific circularity of any moral argument rooted in the appeal to God or the scriptures. Why is X wrong? Because

God says it is. Why does God say it is wrong? Because it just is. Why is it just wrong? Because God says it is! There is, in this argument, no logical reason invoked as to why God might consider X to be wrong. He just does! According to this argument it could be (in theory) a mortal sin to enjoy knitting, just because God says that knitting is morally wrong. So we have to go behind the 'because God says so' argument to discover why it might be that God should consider certain human actions to be right or wrong, and this opens up the possibility that our predecessors (who largely ploughed the 'because God says so' furrow, which can all too easily reflect human and not divine prejudice) may actually have been in error. Once 'because God says so' is shown to be an inadequate ground for ethics, a whole new realm of life-affirming and dynamic ethical possibilities is opened up as we shall see further in subsequent chapters.

The fifth and final difficulty with any straightforward appeal to scripture is that even in dialogue with (and indeed even when it has largely felt itself to be under) the witness of scripture, the church can and does change its mind on what actually constitutes moral behaviour, especially when the issues concerned are ones which we commonly think of as scriptural but which may, on closer examination, turn out to be entirely peripheral to scripture. A prime example would be that of marriage. Those who seek to make scripture a final arbiter (The Irish Fellowship of Evangelical Clergy among them) frequently call for a return to Christian and biblical standards in marriage, by which they mean, essentially, a move away from cohabitation and sex before marriage and towards what one might regard as the traditional norms. Biblical authority is readily invoked, but it is an empty invocation in this case, in that whilst the bible gives plenty of examples of what behaviour inside marriage should be like, it nowhere dictates what actually constitutes a Christian marriage, and in fact what is considered to be a Christian marriage is actually a very recent phenomenon dating from about the sixteenth century, prior to which cohabitation and a promise of faithfulness were considered by both society and the church to constitute a valid marriage.

A similar shift has occurred, at least within Anglicanism, on the subject of contraception. Lambeth 1938 frowned upon it and the spectre of the sin of Onan loomed on the fringes as a biblical warrant for suspicion, but how many Anglicans today would identify with this particular piece of biblical interpretation? Like it or not, the implications are clear: both our interpretation of scripture and with it our ethics have changed and are potentially therefore open to further change in the future. A largely negative ethic may once have been written on tablets of stone, but for a more positive ethical framework this is no longer possible.

In sum, then, what these objections to, and difficulties with a straightforward (and often largely unthinking) appeal to scripture establish is that just as we cannot pin down God, so too, by definition we cannot pin down what this un-pin-downable God is supposed to like or dislike merely through the pages of scripture – which is, anyway, just the record of our ongoing struggle to understand anything at all of God, rather than a divine blueprint for everything.

All of these difficulties and objections are directed against the founding principles of much of traditional Christian ethics, but a series of other and equally cogent objections can be directed at the negative effect which this narrow and inflexible system of ethics has on many devout Christians. To put it bluntly, much of traditional Christian ethics can be interpreted as an edifice designed to make the conforming majority feel comfortable – although whether it is even successful in this may be questioned, as we shall see – and to ensure that those who do not conform (and my argument is that conformity may be a greater motive force in this system than morality) are made to feel suitably guilty and marginalised, thus further reinforcing the feelings of superiority of those who conform. Those who are right know that they are, and those who are wrong are left with little defence or room for argument in a system which, it may be argued, is designed primarily to ensure social conformity rather than genuine morality.

The first and most obvious group of victims of this brutally black and white system of ethics – and certainly in the realm of sexuality with which we are primarily concerned here – has been those who have not conformed to the prevailing moral climate and whose lifestyle has marked them out as 'deviant'. Who these people are has varied somewhat from generation to generation – a fact not without its own significance as we shall consider shortly. No more than a couple of generations ago, then, the primary transgressors were probably reducible to three distinct and equally visible groups: cohabitees, single mothers, and divorcees. All were considered to be beyond any and every social and moral pale, and their treatment by both society and the church underlined their status as outcasts. Divorcees and cohabitees would find themselves ostracised by at least some of their family and acquaintance; divorcees were never permitted to remarry in church; and both groups would find themselves – certainly in the Roman Catholic Church and not infrequently in the Anglican Church – effectively excommunicated. Probably the worst treatment was, however, reserved for single mothers, and here the scope for moral opprobrium and degradation was almost endless: severe pressure to give up a child for adoption, the Magdalen laundries, and even asylums were the fate of those unfortunate enough to break this social and religious taboo.

All of this would have been cruel enough even if the moral standards invoked could have been shown to be inviolably 'right' and eternally unchanging. But the ultimate cruelty of this system of ethics, however, is that those standards were not of this timeless and absolute kind. Quite simply, we have, over the past fifty years or so, largely changed our minds, and the intolerable treatment of thousands of people in past generations is now shown to be rooted only in a passing social mores and prejudice rather than in anything more substantial. This fact – that both society and the church can change their minds on supposedly moral issues – should, in the future, make us very wary indeed of consigning whole segments of society (as, for example, homosexuals and lesbians) to outcast status or judging them to be guilty of a moral lapse just because such and such a set of standards happens to be the accepted norm of any one society or church. If it is not again to be indiscriminately cruel, Christian ethics must have a genuine rationale behind it and not rest on any naïve and simplistic set of supposed *a priori* moral absolutes which, it is claimed, just 'are'.

If these groups of people, such as cohabitees, divorces and single mothers, are the primary ones to have been hurt by an unjust and cruel system of ethics, then the other major group consists of most of the rest of us, who have been less obviously and overtly but no less far-reachingly affected by it. The insidious effects of our ethics have been two-fold. First, as Don Cupitt and others have rightly observed, these ethics have inculcated a form of 'school rules' mentality in many Christians, the effect of which is to produce a 'don't blot your copybook' and 'keep your head down' ethos, rather than a more positive and outgoing approach to ethics. Ethics – and with it the whole of the Christian life – is seen as being about not doing wrong rather than about a positive doing of good, and certainly so in the area of sexuality.

Secondly, this ultra-conservative and negative approach has inhibited people from fully enjoying and rejoicing in their own bodies and their own sexuality. Victorian Puritanism has reacted with the ever-present catalyst of original sin (and guilt) to make Christians especially fear and repress their sexuality and to mistrust their own bodies, feeling them to be much more a potential cause of sin than a potential channel of grace, rejoicing or holiness. For many faithful Christians (until society changed its sexual rules regardless of the church, and perhaps even since this change also) the potential richness of their sexuality has been mistrusted and stamped down, and the old Victorian joke adage of 'Once a week is ample' has ceased to sound quite so funny.

The effects of this fear-inspired repression of sexuality are more far-reaching than might at first seem obvious, since they encompass the whole person and not merely the specific area of sexuality. That is, dissatisfaction with one's sexuality will tend to lead to a dissatisfaction with oneself. Human beings are notoriously efficient at hoovering up ideas of sin and guilt, and, given the history of Christianity and its track record on the issue, sexuality is a prime area for inculcating these feelings. Thus, even if we are 'modern' enough to take on board the findings of the sex-researchers of the mid to late twentieth century, and liberated enough to admit to enjoying certain things which earlier generations might have frowned upon, there is still for many people an inherent guilt (however unfounded) which is the price of their pleasure. This feeling of guilt can then eat into other areas of life and lead to a sense of overall dissatisfaction with oneself, a lessening of self-worth, or a feeling of wishing that one were different from how one actually is. And all of these feelings are negative and destructive to the overall quality of life and relationships, and again are founded upon nothing more than the arbitrary 'just because' rules which are our inheritance in the realm of sexuality.

The ultimate effect of all of this is one which surely runs counter to the intention of any truly moral system of ethics, this effect being that of the systematic suppression or downplaying of many manifestations of human love. For many people – and not just those who step outside whatever the accepted social and 'moral' conventions of any particular time might be – life, in the realm of sensuality and especially sexuality, has been hemmed in and circumscribed, and people have for generations been afraid to express their passionate natures lest society (and with it the God which it has largely assumed to be in its own image) should frown on them. Sexuality has become an area in which, again to quote the 1662 marriage service, the 'avoidance of sin' rather than any celebration of human loving has become paramount, and the effect is at once deadening and guilt-imparting, not only as far as sexuality itself is concerned, but throughout the domain of the potentially warmer and passionate and creatively self-expressive side of human life.

Our inheritance of Christian ethics, then, is flawed on two counts: in many of its supposedly unchanging principles, which boil down to nothing more than a divine version of 'because I say so', and in its detrimental effects upon the human psyche,

our comfort with our own bodies, and the ability of human beings to express their fundamentally loving natures.

In the face of this legacy, therefore, it is at last time to find a
new starting point for ethics which is neither so inflexible as that
which we have inherited, nor at the same time, as prone to the
disease of relativism as systems such as 'situation ethics' tend to
be. What is needed is a foundation which will provide ethical
guidelines, but which will do so in a less cruel and often arbitrary way than has usually been the case hitherto. Such a starting point is one which will be based not in negative rules, but in
a search for the inspiration towards creative and loving behaviour and values, values which may in themselves help us to re-
evaluate and perhaps even re-define our constrained and often
cruel notions of 'right' and 'wrong'. It is to the identification of
this starting point that we must now turn.

CHAPTER SIX

Towards Creativity in Ethics

In previous chapters we have established that God is more un-
known and more passible than metaphysics has usually allowed
him/her to be, and we have argued that ethics needs to become
more flexible and creative and cease to make any appeal to a set
of pre-packaged and supposedly divine rules. The starting point
for such an ethics must not continue to rest in any sort of circular
appeal to scripture or in spurious claims to certainty as to what
God wants, but in whatever it is that we can (however falteringly)
begin to know about God, both from our considered reflection
on scripture (rather than a naïve and absolute appeal to it), and
from our own experience of God and our fundamental convictions about the nature of God stemming from the evidence of the
universe in which we live, and God's activity – with whatever
clarity we may perceive this – within it.

Given that we can no longer plausibly construct ethics on a
'because God says so' basis, what are the attributes of God to
which we might appeal in order to find a starting place for ethics
without falling back into any sort of naïve or literalist appeal to
scripture? In essence I suggest that there are two such attributes
which, however ineffable God may be held to be, are nonetheless known to us because they are witnessed to not only in scripture but also in God's dealings with creation and specifically
with humanity. These attributes therefore – rather than a somewhat randomly selected set of rules – represent a viable starting
place for any discussion of our relationship with God and our
understanding of what God's demands upon us might be. These
two attributes, then, are first God's creativity, and secondly,
God's love.

That God is creative seems to be almost the first thing which must rightly be said of him/her, although it is important to establish that this is not the same as appealing to any variety of fundamentalist creationism. Yes, the Book of Genesis speaks in beautiful and poetic myth of God as creative, but we do not have to take this picture in any way literally: rather, God's creativity is extrapolated from the combined 'facts' of belief in God and the existence of anything at all. In other words, if God is believed to exist at all then it is reasonable also to believe that this God is responsible, in some way or another, for the existence of all that is. We may not know exactly how God exercises this creativity through the billions of years since whatever 'big bang' brought the universe into being and through the endless permutations of selection in evolution since then, but we may, without falling into fundamentalism, assert that God has been creatively at work in all of this.

If all of this is allowed, and God is acknowledged as present and working in the creation by whatever means, then this immediately establishes two important benchmarks as far as both the act of creativity and the creation itself (and ourselves within it, therefore) are concerned. It establishes, if we believe in the goodness of God and his actions, first that creativity is a genuine moral good: that is, the act of creation is good in itself and the results of that creativity are therefore themselves good, an idea which is reflected in the lovely picture-book language of Genesis where the narrator has God concluding each 'day' of creation by reflecting, 'and behold God saw that it was good'.

In addition to this it also provides a warrant for claiming that our own rootedness in creation makes our essential bodily nature good, and again the same picture stories in Genesis have the enhanced refrain at the end of the sixth 'day' (when the world was peopled), 'and behold God saw that it was very good'. A genuinely strong doctrine of God's creativity suggests that embodiedness is good, and not, as many of the ascetics of the first four centuries or so believed, something devoutly to be regretted! Indeed, as I have hinted in other places, it is probably high time that contemporary Christianity had a major argument with some of the chief figures of those centuries and knocked them off their pedestals and undid, or at least attempted to repair, some of the immense damage which they have inflicted upon the Christian world. It is about time that we believed fully and wholeheartedly in the innate goodness of the creation – and ourselves and our bodies – and did away with such things as the Augustinian nonsense of not merely original sin but original guilt. This is not to deny human sin which is very real, but rather to say that it is not – as Christianity has so often seemed to say – the primary defining feature of humanity. That primary defining feature is instead a goodness which is shared with the whole of creation: that is the essence of humanity, however much we may individually and corporately mar it through sin.

If creativity is the first attribute to which our experience of God bears witness, then love is the ultimate attribute of God which manifests itself to us, and again, if we believe, as we claim to, certain things, then this establishes a further series of reference points for our understanding of ourselves, our relationship with God, and the ways in which we might begin to do ethics. The initial impact of this emphasis on the divine love is that we are enabled to see the presence of creation, and our presence within it, as the direct outcome of the love expressed in creation. It was love which willed creation into being, and our presence here – even if mediated by millions of years of evolution – is God's own loving wish. This love was then taken even further, in that it not only willed us into being but then also spoke to us and redeemed us in Jesus Christ. Our Incarnational faith proclaims that we are loved and reached out to as who we are. And thirdly, it is, we believe, God's will that we should be with him for all eternity through resurrection to eternal life: we are, as lovingly created and lovingly redeemed creatures, loveable enough in God's eyes for our presence with him/her for eternity to be both willed and desired.

These two attributes of creativity and love are not ones which are read off arbitrarily from the pages of scripture or which rely on a 'because God or the bible says so' rationale. Rather, they are both ones which are of the essence of our belief about God and which have been borne witness to by the experience of countless Christians throughout the ages. They are indeed foundational: if we cannot believe that God is creative and loving then very few of the other more complicated and sophisticated beliefs which we have will either matter or indeed make any sense at all. This is not metaphysical speculation, but the bedrock of faith. What these two attributes do in the context of the present argument, then, is to offer us a non-metaphysical and flexible starting point for an ethics which is rooted in the nature of God him/herself. By positing these two over-arching characteristics as being of the essence of divinity, God is not thereby narrowed down into a cosmic dictator with a rigid set of rules, and nor are we allowed to assume that we simply 'know' what God wants. Instead they are a starting point, but one from which, thereafter, we have to think and pray our way into ethics.

The primary purpose of this book is to explore some of the connections between doctrine and ethics, between how we conceive of God and the way in which this affects our whole conception of ethics. It is in this sense a prolegomenon to the creation of a detailed system of ethics which is a further and separate task. My intention here is not to delve too far into the minutiae of ethics, but rather, in more general terms to outline what our ethics might plausibly begin to look like, given certain of our beliefs about, and experiences of, God. In this chapter, then, I do not propose to work fully through the development of a full ethical system, but rather to make certain points about such a system and to pose a series of questions which might make for a fruitful ongoing discussion.

As we begin to look directly at the sphere of ethics, then, probably the most important observation to make at the outset is that, as should have become apparent by now, I am proposing to start doing ethics from a quite different place from that which is usually employed. Most thinking about ethics begins from some sort of concepts of 'right' and 'wrong' – whether God-given, rooted in the so called 'natural' order or whatever. Such a jump-ing-off point is not, I believe, in the end helpful because, as I have already argued at length, it fails to go to the heart of why things are right or wrong, but merely assumes that they just 'are'. Indeed, in a sense, the concepts of 'right' and 'wrong' are probably the last ones which any ethical system should identify, rather than, as so often, the first ones.

By way of a minor digression, though an entirely topical one, this is, I believe, one of the central dilemmas which will have faced the Lambeth Commission for the past year or so. Admittedly its terms of reference are more to do with how to live with diversity and with the nature and limits of commu-nion, rather than specifically to do with the debate about homo-sexual clergy. However, it is difficult to imagine that there will have been no discussion of this issue which, after all, gave rise to the need for the commission in the first place, and if that discus-sion begins with the supposed ethics of the matter then it is hard to see how it will not have degenerated into a kind of "'Tis', "'Tisn't' argument, no matter how cleverly and eruditely dressed up it may have been. Here, surely, is a prime instance of what I am advocating: namely, that doctrine and the grounds for any ethics should be the place to start, and that the overtly ethi-cal discussions should at all costs be left until last when at least something of the 'why' of ethics might by then have been ad-dressed.

To return, though, to the matter in hand: I am proposing that serious consideration be given by the church to the development of a new model of Christian ethics which is based on the princi-ples of divine (and therefore also of human) creativity and love; and I am proposing also that these principles are (or should be) the touchstones which will provide the logic according to which we will form conclusions as to the acceptability or otherwise of particular actions.

Such an ethics might have profound consequences, not least in the area of sexuality with which we have been primarily con-cerned in this study. It might, for example, because it does not define every act as definitively right or wrong according to a pre-existent set of rules, allow much more of the range of human sexual loving to be seen altogether more positively, in that it would make it possible to see human sexual loving as one supreme expression of reaching out and self-giving, which, in some senses at least (such as the offering of self and one's consequent vulnerability) is analogous to the depth of divine self-giving in creation and redemption. Furthermore, if this is the case, then it is likely that an ethic developed along these lines would be more open and affirming, healing rather than pain-inflicting, more demarginalising and inclusive than so much of traditional Christian ethics has been. We shall return to consider these points more fully in subsequent chapters, but it is important here at least simply to note these possibilities, however briefly.

Furthermore, in the light of these possibilities and of a radically different ethical standpoint from which to consider sexuality, might we (to concentrate for a moment on the issue of homosexuality) even be able as a church, to bring ourselves to think that a committed, stable and loving homosexual or lesbian relationship which is life affirming to the two people involved and to those around them is simply 'wrong' no longer? That it might even, within an ethics of creativity and love, be seen as a creative and loving choice? Or at least, even if such a sea-change remains still some way off, might a new approach to ethics mean that there might be a great deal more room for constructive discussion (and listening) than just the firing of proof texts and equally vehement denial of them, which is so often all that this particular debate succeeds in generating at the present?

Whatever the future may hold in terms of this particular debate, there is a cogent case to be made for the idea that the church's thinking on ethics in the realm of sexuality in particular is overdue for a change, and a radical one. Such a change would be initiated by rooting ethics more firmly in doctrine, as I have indicated here: doctrine has an inbuilt flexibility in the face of the ultimate mystery of God and ethics needs to come to share that flexibility. There are new and creative possibilities for ethical thinking, and the church should not be afraid of venturing to try them: the church can and does change its mind, as we have seen, and we are not necessarily in thrall for ever to Augustine and his gloomy view of sex and human nature.

In advocating this ethical re-think I am not, at this relatively early stage in the discussion, even claiming that the approach I have outlined is necessarily the right one, but merely that it, or something like it, deserves a great deal of thought on the part of the church if it wishes to open up new approaches, attitudes and lines of thought in a debate which is otherwise threatening to harden attitudes on all sides to the point of petrifaction.

Finally, before we proceed in the next chapters to explore further how an ethics of creativity and loving might impinge both upon our experience of our own sexuality and on our spirituality and relationship with God, it is important to add two crucial footnotes to this manner of thinking ethically, which attempt respectively first to pre-empt one possible objection to it, and secondly to withdraw the option of simply ignoring the pressing need for change by posing as an ethical ostrich with one's head firmly in the sand!

First, then, although it does not start from them it is important to make it very clear that an ethics based on love and creativity does not do away with the concepts of 'right' and 'wrong': that is, it does not lead to a vague and woolly 'anything goes' kind of mentality. On the contrary, the effect of choosing a different starting point is actually to refine (and perhaps even to some extent to re-define) our ideas of right and wrong by providing a much less arbitrary (and much more doctrinally centred) basis for why we decide that certain things are right or wrong. For example, murder and adultery do not suddenly become morally acceptable as a result of a slide into some sort of anarchic moral relativism, but in an ethics of creativity and love they are considered to be wrong not because of any divine fiat but because they are destructive of life, love or relationships. It cannot be stressed often enough that this approach to ethics is not a soft option or a cop-out.

Secondly, whilst all may not agree with the precise nature of the views expressed here, nonetheless the need for ethical revision and a renewed exploration of the close links between ethics and doctrine can hardly be ignored. For, whatever any individual may make of the content of my particular argument, it remains true that neither metaphysics (which is only pictures anyway) nor the bible itself allows us to arrive at the ultra-certain position of 'because God says so' or 'because the bible says so'. Ethics is linked to doctrine, and our doctrine is a great deal more complex than assuming (or claiming) that we have got God cornered; and if doctrine is more tentative than perhaps has often been imagined, then so too will (and should) be our ethics, which might also serve to make those same ethics more creative and less cruel than Christian history has so often found them to be.

CHAPTER SEVEN

Sexuality and Holiness

In the course of thinking about and writing this book, it has become increasingly clear that if we are successfully to re-negotiate the relationship between doctrine and ethics, and the Christian understanding of sexual ethics in particular, then there are two quite distinct but clearly related tasks to be undertaken: the legacy of the past must be substantially undone and a way forward forged for the future. Hitherto in this study we have largely been concerned with the first of these tasks. Thus we have argued against the constraints of traditional metaphysics, of scriptural literalism, and of arbitrary and inflexible ethical codes derived from a supposed divine fiat. The purpose of all this is a little like the clearing of ground before planting or the demolition of a ruin before re-building. There is little point in either planting or building without such preliminary work as the results will be infiltrated and compromised by the legacy of the past. Similarly with ethics, it is simply not possible to build for the future without first dismantling at least some of the past – the general atmosphere of negativity surrounding sexuality needs to be thoroughly dispelled before there can be any positive future developments. It is my contention that we have shown this entrenched negativity to be unfounded in doctrine and therefore in ethics, and that we are not thereby bound by the body-fearing repression of sexuality which we have inherited from the first five or six centuries of Christian history and which has been reinforced at regular intervals ever since.

As a fulcrum between this task and the succeeding one we have, then, in the previous chapter begun at least to sketch in a new vision for Christian ethics, a vision rooted firmly in doctrine and looking to the attributes of God for its foundations rather than, in the first instance, to the notoriously inflexible and human value-laden concepts of right and wrong.

It is, therefore, in this atmosphere of ethical fresh air that we can begin to look towards the future and to creative and fulfilling possibilities for Christian sexual ethics. That is, we can now begin to explore the ways in which sexuality (in its many diverse forms) might be seen to be not only not evil (the first part of the task) but also a genuine and positive moral good which might even have an enriching and beneficial influence upon our spiritual lives also.

And so we come to the second part of our task which is, in a sense, encapsulated in the title of this chapter – the effort to make connections between our human nature as sexual beings and our quest for holiness and participation in the holiness of God him/herself.

At first sight, the linking of the two terms 'sexuality' and 'holiness' probably seems – given our upbringing and heritage within the church – to be at best a contradiction in terms and at worst tantamount to blasphemy. In the conventional wisdom of the church, they sit together about as comfortably as kippers and custard or Archdeacons and salvation! Indeed within that fear-ridden conventional wisdom they are opposing terms – sexuality with its immense power being seen as a force which threatens to draw us away from the higher spiritual realms into the lower (and potentially morally dubious) carnal ones.

What is proposed here, though, is a precise reversal of these presuppositions as to the relationship between the bodily (including the sexual) and the spiritual. Where once our bodies were seen to drag us downward – away from God and towards sin – I shall argue the exact reverse, namely, that our bodily and sexual nature may be a powerful means of grace, that it may in fact be a God-given faculty through which we are enabled to transcend ourselves and discover within ourselves at least some of the qualities, including something of the love, of God himself.

The basis of this claim is the founding of ethics in the experi-

enced nature of God as being pre-eminently one of creativity
and love. If this is the case, and if we can argue that our sexuality
shares in some degree these divinely originating values, then we
will be in a strong position to argue for the potential holiness
(and not merely the 'un-badness') of our sexuality.

There is, however, one final piece of ground-clearing to be
done. Hopefully we will by now have jettisoned some of the
baggage surrounding sexuality and the ideas of right and
wrong, but we have now entered the realm of holiness and this
too carries a heavy weight of association (and misconception)
deriving from the first few centuries of Christian thought.

Thus mention the word 'holiness' in almost any Christian
gathering and a wealth of ideas and images will spring to mind,
and the chances are that these ideas and images will be ones
which largely distance ninety-nine percent of all Christians from
any hope of ever achieving holiness. The notions which most
usually surround the concept of holiness are those of set-apart-
ness, dispassionateness, unworldliness, disinterestedness and
so on. Holiness is that which draws us apart from the realm of
everyday activities and encourages us to let go of our earthly
and earthbound nature and ascend (purely by means of spiritual
exercises or resources) nearer to God, who is, of course, pure
Spirit. Holiness thus understood involves in some way a leaving
behind of that which makes us most obviously and identifiably
ourselves – that is, our bodies. Still the body-defying ascetics of
the early centuries are having the last laugh (or at least the
penultimate one) as far as our understanding of holiness is concerned.

But the question may pertinently be asked, is this conception
of holiness really holiness or is it, for the most part, escapism? Is
it a wish that we were not who we are (that is, embodied) and an
attempt to reach God without reference to who we really are? Is
it – if this is indeed the case – not itself a form of blasphemy, or at
least a rejection of God, in that it is a denial of our true nature
and a negation of God's own creative handiwork?

Thankfully (as with sexuality as we have seen in Chapter

Four) there is a contrary, although less dominant stream in the Christian tradition to which we may appeal for our understanding of holiness, and one which allows for our embodiedness to be a genuine potential part of our holiness. Thus, just as we have applied to the medieval mystics to redeem our use of sexual imagery and metaphor in the spiritual life, so too (doubtless amongst others) we may appeal to the Celtic church to rehabilitate our notions of what constitutes the holy. That said, one caveat must be entered before any such appeal can be entertained: Celtic spirituality is a growth industry at present, and there is more than enough romanticisation and quasi-Celtic plagiarism around, much of which is of dubious worth and very uncertain quality. Underneath all of this, however, there does seem to be a genuinely identifiable strain of Celtic spirituality, and it is one which profoundly links – and indeed intertwines, in the manner of the Celtic knot-work designs – the realms of the holy and the everyday. Within the best of Celtic spirituality, then, is a sense that the holy is not set totally apart from the here and now, but indwells it and is indwelt by it. And hence comes, for all the romanticisations of such prayers, the genuine provenance of prayers for ordinary earthy everyday activities such as milking the cows, lighting and banking up the fire and so on. It is this sense of encounter with the extraordinary in the ordinary, the transcendent in the immanent, that is one of the hallmarks of Celtic spirituality, and one to which the paying of some attention may richly repay us today in the present context.

So, then, in the light of this counter-culture, and contrary to the body/sexuality/life denying tenor of so much of our tradition, what is holiness and how might we begin to relate it positively to our experience of ourselves as embodied and sexual beings? For the contemporary mind it is almost impossible to enter upon any discussion of holiness without invoking the name of Rudolf Otto, whose magisterial work *The Idea of the Holy* has, since 1923, largely shaped our ideas on the subject. Probably Otto's most important key concept in this book is the idea of the holy as the 'numinous', as the *mysterium tremendum et fascinans*.

It is all too easy to see this as being primarily to do with the 'apartness' of the holy, its distance from us, and the reverence and indeed fear which we must feel in its presence. Certainly this is part of the picture of holiness and one which scripture bears a rich witness to in such episodes as Moses not being allowed to see the face of God, and the bearer of the Ark of the Covenant touching the holy (with the best of intentions!) and dropping dead.

It is, however, important to stress that there is another and equally important dimension to the holy, and this is the fact that even as we are amazed and awed by it we are also irresistibly drawn on by it. As Eric James has put it, holiness at once 'knocks us back and draws us on'. Holiness and the holy are not simply remote from us and states to which we aspire with varying degrees of hopelessness. Instead the holy is something which is actively reaching out towards us and searching us out. That this is so is powerfully borne out in our experience both of holy people and holy places. Most of us have had the good fortune to encounter at least a small number of people whom we would describe as truly holy, and a common feature of many such people is an almost transparent attractiveness of character. They may be of very different personality types, but there is a common core of integrity, warmth, love, goodness or whatever which exercises its own unique attraction. It may be that we wish to be with them, or it may be that we wish to become more like them, but either way there is a sense of being reached out to and perhaps even enveloped by holiness. Similarly with holy places. Very often one will enter a church or other holy site and be struck by an almost tangible sense of the presence of goodness, devoutness and even divinity. It is as if the building is peopled with the holiness of those who have worshipped there before (a sense in T. S. Eliot's immortal phrase, of kneeling 'where prayer has been valid'), and again there may well be a consciousness of being drawn into and perhaps changed by that atmosphere of holiness.

But holiness is an even more everyday-based quality than

this might suggest. Our pattern for holiness must presumably, as Christians, be Jesus himself, and his holiness was not a world-eschewing or eremitic and introspective thing. Certainly he is recorded on a substantial number of occasions as going apart to pray, often up a hillside, but this more private and reserved dimension of personal spirituality is only a tiny fragment of the whole revelation of and encounter with the holiness of Jesus. Rather than alone up a hillside, I would argue that the primary locus of Jesus' holiness is in his encounters with other people, and specifically and supremely in the depth of his self-giving love for others. As evidence of this we may look naturally to the crucifixion – an absolute giving of life for others – but there is a host of other instances recorded in the gospels in which Jesus gives of himself profoundly on behalf of those around him. There is, clearly, all the teaching and healing, and within this there are also moments when Jesus is taken by surprise by someone's depth of need or faith and responds – even when distracted from some prior purpose – with compassion and healing; the Syro-Phoenecian woman and the woman suffering from bleeding who touched his cloak are excellent examples of this. In addition to this there is the depth of his compassion and longing for the wholeness of the other which shines through many of Jesus' conversations with the people he met. We may think here of the rich young man or the Samaritan woman at the well, for example, and regardless of the particular verbal historicity of these specific incidents it is highly likely that Jesus is recorded in this kind of way because it does faithfully reflect something of the way in which he responded to the people whom he encountered. Furthermore, and still in addition to the ultimate self-giving of the crucifixion, there is the fact that, if we may believe not necessarily the letter but rather the general tenor of the gospel records, Jesus never turned away any who came to him. He may have argued with and rebuked those who tried to trap him, but for all who came in good faith or in genuine need there was a welcome and a personal encounter in response to their need or questions. Indeed, the gospels record the disciples as attempting to send a variety of people away – children and a blind man to identify but a couple of instances – and Jesus overruling them. The primary locus then, of Jesus' holiness is the openness and selflessness with which he encounters others, at whatever cost of time, strength, power (and ultimately life) to himself.

That this should be so is unqualified good news as far as our understanding of our own holiness (and our ability to achieve it) is concerned. For it is given to relatively few of us, either by nature, opportunity or vocation, to achieve a holiness of a contemplative monastic variety in which days are regularly punctuated by hours of corporate and private worship and meditation. While speaking of monasticism, though, it is worth noting that even this apparently inward-looking holiness almost always finds an outworking in self-giving, through teaching, counselling, nursing and so on, and indeed the Abbot of one entirely closed order told me years ago that although his monks did none of these things, yet their existence in that enclosed order was not primarily for themselves but 'for the world which stands in need of prayer'. Even an enclosed holiness is ultimately one of self-giving in its regular discipline of prayer for others. For the vast majority of us, however, life is lived and our prayers are prayed firmly out in the everyday world and alongside other people, at home, at school, at work, at church, in the pub or the sports club or the supermarket. And it is, consequently, here that our holiness must be achieved and must bear the fruit of a more richly-graced world.

Thus we are led to the question: in what does our holiness of everyday most properly consist? And for answer we return to the pattern of our own holiness, Jesus, and look for the making real of his self-offering and self-giving in our lives such that we can re-present (and therefore represent) Christ in the world of our own time and place. There is no room here for the caricature of holiness which so often does duty for the real thing – a pious, indeed sanctimonious bearing which looks down from a lofty height on the frailties and follies of the world, not reaching out to the need of the world but keeping its hands (metaphorically

at least) folded in prayer all the while. This caricature of holiness
– all too familiar not only from TV 'vicars' but also in real life –
seems to understand holiness as an attitude or a quality: on the
contrary, I suggest, holiness is not so much a quality as an activity. Holiness is not so much about *what we are* as about *what we
do*. This is not for a moment to deny that holiness is also rooted
in our prayer, worship, private meditation, reflection on scripture and so on, but merely to say that these things do not of
themselves constitute holiness unless they issue in a self-giving
reaching out towards the world both in prayer and in action.
There is, as there has been since the epistles of St James and St
Paul, a tension between 'faith' and 'works' as it were, but without at all denying the internal spiritual dimension of our own
prayer life, it is equally vital to assert that holiness, understood
fully, is not some sort of self-reflexive inward-looking achievement, but a grace which is fed by our prayers and which results
in turn in the gracing of others through our self-offering.

Learning to define, or even re-define holiness correctly in a
way which recognises its outward as much as its inward aspects
is, I think, essential to the process of re-integrating our sexuality
with our spirituality and with finding a place for it within a re-
thought framework of doctrine and ethics. If holiness is defined
as an inward or attitudinal state, then the sheer physicality of
sexuality plainly sits very uncomfortably alongside it; once holiness is admitted to have an active dimension, then it may be that
our bodies – and with them our sexuality – are enabled to become part of that holiness and to reflect its characteristics in
even the most obviously physical dimension of our lives.

A claim such as this obviously needs to be fleshed out (if that is
the appropriate phrase!) somewhat, and I propose therefore to
explore at least briefly four ways in which our sexuality has the
potential to share some of the qualities of holiness and also to share
in some of the qualities which we have dwelt on in previous chapters in looking at God's nature as being one of creativity and love.

First, then, there is in our sexual loving a genuine sense of
reaching-out beyond ourselves to another and, importantly, the

needs of the other are put before our own. Sex is not about a self-ish self-satisfaction, but about mutuality and giving. There is a continuous process of adjusting to, and reading the body-language of one's partner, and there is, I venture to suggest, an even greater delight in pleasure given than received. In a sense, sexual loving is about not merely reaching out to another person, but also existing primarily for the other rather than for oneself. Perhaps even more closely resonating with echoes of the language of holiness is the fact that one of the primary purposes of this reaching out is not to communicate our own demands but to enable us to become 'in tune' with the desires/needs/wishes of our partner. There is at least an echo here of the openness to the will of another with which we come (or at least should come) both to prayer and to the practice of holiness in everyday living.

Secondly, and flowing from this activity of reaching out, there is in our sexuality – and especially in our physical expression of it – a genuine sense of self-giving. Yes, of course it is possible, and regrettably I am sure that in all sorts of contexts it happens too often, to engage in sex without either reaching out or giving, but I am talking here of our sexuality in its best expressions rather than its least loving, and therefore, in the terms of our argument, least moral ones. For in true sexual loving there is a real self-offering and giving. There is a real feeling of the giving away of ourselves and the putting of ourselves (quite literally) in the hands of another.

This is plainly true physically, but it is just as true emotionally – and again I would stress that I am speaking of sexual loving at its most committed and therefore at its most moral. When we give ourselves physically to another human being this is, in a sense, simply a reflection of the fact that we have already given them all of who we are emotionally anyway. Our feelings, thoughts, desires, wishes, fears and so on are already in our partner's care, and the act of offering our body equally into their care and love is simply an extension of (as well, perhaps, as an intensification and a physical manifestation of) an emotional giving which has already taken place.

Alongside this self-giving, and stemming directly from it, comes the third sense in which sexuality can mirror our holiness and even our understanding of God, and that is the sheer vulnerability to which our sexuality can expose us. We have seen the vulnerability of God expressed in creation and in redemptive love – vulnerable simply to our rejection of God's gifts and loving nature – and in our self-giving holiness we are equally vulnerable to those who would reject our offering of ourselves. Similarly our sexuality exposes us to the possibility of hurt or rejection, and the more open and honest our loving the greater the risk we take and the more complete therefore is our vulnerability.

It is important too that, just as with our self-giving, our vulnerability is not simply physical but emotional as well. Certainly we are vulnerable physically, and not merely to rejection or rebuff, but also to the times when – whether male or female – our bodies, for whatever reason, let us down and threaten to humiliate us by their non-responsiveness, which can also, of course conversely look all too easily like a rejection from our partner's standpoint. But even more centrally and powerfully, our sexuality opens up our emotional vulnerability. For on the whole there is no-one to whom we are more open and vulnerable than our partner, and this is not restricted to those occasions when our sexuality is being in any way overtly expressed, and yet it is the 'totality' of this sexual relationship which is one of the major factors in creating this vulnerability. Thus we may, for example, argue with a wide variety of people, but it is the argument with our partner which hurts the most; we may feel annoyed by the disapproval of others, but the disapproval of our partner is likely to be experienced as impinging at some level upon our self-identity and self-worth, and so on. Our physical openness to one another is mirrored (indeed, preceded) by a corresponding emotional openness, and this openness and consequent vulnerability of the whole person once again reflects God's own vulnerability in his dealings with creation. Our sexual loving reflects at least something of the experience of the divine loving in its dependence upon the response of the other if it is to be complete and reciprocal and not fractured and disappointed.

Fourthly, and in a way coming full circle and returning to and yet deepening our starting point of reaching out, our sexuality through its self-giving and vulnerability is able to lead us to a sense of what might be called 'ultimate encounter'. By this I mean a relationship which has no reserve and no hiding, but which is instead a total and completely reciprocal relationship. In such a relationship there is a sense of being 'taken out' of ourselves, of losing ourselves, of, indeed, transcendence. In our deepest loving we leave behind our fears, inadequacies and self-dissatisfaction and experience both ourselves and our partner as simply 'being' – there is indeed almost a sense of ontological simplicity and rightness, or at least givenness, about the expression of our committed sexual loving. Rowan Williams very beautifully captures something of this sense of completeness and giving of true sexual loving when he writes:

> In sexual relation I am no longer in charge of what I am. Any genuine experience of desire leaves me in something like this position: I cannot of myself satisfy my wants without distorting or trivialising them. But here we have a particularly intense case of the helplessness of the ego alone. For my body to be the cause of joy, the end of homecoming, for me, it must be there for someone else, be perceived, accepted, nurtured; and that means being given over to the creation of joy in that other, because only as directed to the enjoyment, the happiness of the other does it become unreservedly lovable. To desire my joy is to desire the joy of the one I desire; my search for enjoyment through the bodily presence of another is a longing to be enjoyed in my body. We are pleased because we are pleasing.

(Rowan Williams, *The Body's Grace*, London, LGCM, 2003.)

I do not wish to push the parallels too far, but it does at least seem to me that if these four elements are characteristic of our sexuality, then there are genuinely reflections here both of the ways of holiness and of the experienced nature of God in creation and redemption. Similarly, I am not going so far as to argue that our sexuality is exactly a way to holiness, but merely that it need not be thought of – as throughout the ages it most usually has been – as being necessarily divorced from holiness, and that our sexuality may indeed provide insights into the fullness of the self-giving of holiness. The expression of our sexuality might actually be a part of, rather than apart from, our holiness.

Finally in this chapter, and almost as a footnote, it should simply be highlighted that we are not here entering the debate as to the morality of particular sexual acts (which we have done earlier and will do again at later points in this study), but merely establishing a principle and laying the foundations of the argument that our sexuality may even be linked to our holiness in a positive rather than a negative fashion. From here we may now go on to consider some other positive aspects of sexuality before returning to examine further (and finally) the implications of all this for our ethics, for our understanding of God, and last but not least for our ecclesiology.

CHAPTER EIGHT

The Fun of it All

The discussion of sexuality in the context of theology (or *vice versa*) suffers from the potential for a double dose of seriousness. I remember years ago watching a television programme about humour across Europe and being assured by a German producer that in Germany they took humour 'very seriously', and a similar danger of an excess of *gravitas* lurks here with sexuality! It is kind of expected that we should do theology with, if not a long, at least a sombre face, and the same expectation appears to be true of any attempt to discuss not so much the practice but the principles of human sexuality. There is a real and ever-present danger that the powerful (and joyous) reality of our sexuality becomes swamped in a miasma of theory, doctrine and ethical speculation.

It is vitally necessary that at some point in the discussion, and now would seem to be as good as any other time, we should remind ourselves of one other central fact about our sexuality and its expression and consider in some detail the implications of this fact – the fact in question being, quite simply, that over and above all supposedly higher or more important considerations, sex is enjoyable: it is fun!

At a fairly basic level this is probably just as well, for if sex were as enthralling as cleaning the sink or as sensually pleasurable as unblocking the drains, then we probably couldn't be bothered! The drive to procreate may be a strong one, but it is at least partly so (and perhaps even almost entirely so) precisely because the means of procreation is pleasurable rather than painful or merely tedious. This suggests very strongly that words such as pleasure, enjoyment, fun, as well as the deeper and more ultimately profound terms explored in the previous chapter are entirely applicable to our sexual activity, and are an essential ingredient of it at least as much as, if not more than, procreation itself.

I am, of course, aware that depending upon one's standpoint this idea will come across as being anywhere along a spectrum from self-evident truth to heresy, and the more conservative one's Christianity (whether Reformed or Roman Catholic) the more procreation is likely to be exalted as the primary, or even the sole legitimate reason for sexual activity. Certainly this would be the traditional norm of most church teaching on sexuality. It is, for example, the implicit teaching of the *Book of Common Prayer Marriage Service* within the Anglican Church, and it is to this day the explicit teaching of the Roman Catholic *magisterium* on the subject of marriage – although it must also be admitted that it is honoured more in the breach than in the observance by increasing numbers of the Roman Catholic faithful.

We have seen, however, already in the course of this study that Christianity is quite capable of changing its mind on matters both of doctrine and ethics, and a substantial case can be made for suggesting that procreation should cease to be regarded as the principal reason for sexual activity, and that other concepts such as pleasure and expression of mutuality should be allowed to exist unashamedly alongside procreation as valid reasons for sex.

In large measure, this case hinges on doing two things: first, not attempting to make either the bible or Christian tradition (and especially the earlier centuries of it) say what they do not say or say what we might wish they had said; and secondly, working towards an understanding of why those societies and traditions came to the conclusions they did and asking, in the light of this, whether those conclusions are necessarily binding for us today.

Clearly, then, we must in the first instance be honest enough to allow both scripture and tradition to say what they say and mean what they mean and, further, be honest enough to admit that this witness is, without exception, firmly opposed to all varieties of non-procreative sex and, perhaps, especially opposed to homosexuality. The scriptural texts, and particularly those from Leviticus and Romans, are all familiar enough and I do not propose to rehearse them again here. Instead I merely note that to the voice of scripture is to be added that of a whole gallery of worthies from the Christian tradition, some of whom we have encountered before in this study, and among the most eminent of these being Augustine and St Thomas Aquinas to name but a couple.

The question at issue then, is not so much what scripture and tradition say, for this is unequivocal, but why they say what they say. Do they do so because of some absolute *a priori* moral reasoning or revelation, or do they do so largely, if not entirely, as a result of the times and societies in which they thought and wrote and the kinds of understandings and concerns which were prevalent in those times and societies? Here I am also acutely aware that we are straying into the issue of the authority of scripture which is a huge topic all of its own, but even at the risk of over-simplifying such a massive subject, it is necessary that we at least broach the debate if we are even to begin to progress our argument in terms of sexuality and morality, for clearly in any such argument the biblical witness must be taken seriously, whatever conclusion we may then reach about this witness.

I have already argued that we are not in any position to read off any comprehensive set of ready-made moral laws – that the nature of God and the problems of metaphysics simply do not give us this luxury – and therefore we must equally conclude that neither was any previous society in such a position, even if reading-off self-evident or revealed moral laws was exactly what they thought they were doing. Unless we are biblical literalists (a position which is intellectually untenable for too many reasons to list here) then we cannot simply assume that God approves or disapproves of certain things simply because a previous generation of believers thought he did, and we are thrown

back again onto the question of *why* they reached the conclusions they did and then, naturally enough, imputed these ideas
also to the God in whom they believed.

In my reflections at this point, I am indebted to Professor
Nigel Biggar for some thoughts expressed in a recent paper
(published in *Search*, Volume 27, Number 3), entitled 'Does the
Faith Stand or Fall Here?' which addresses the whole realm of
sexuality, with specific reference to the contemporary Anglican
debates on homosexuality and the authority of scripture.

In answer to the question of why the scriptural writers (and
following them the emerging Christian tradition) thought as
they did, the response would appear to be two-fold – that they
thought as they did partly as a result of their understanding of
human biology, and partly as a result of the respective positions
of Israelite society, and to a lesser extent the emerging early
Christian society, for much of the biblical period.

The first factor, then, which would appear to be responsible
for the biblical writers thinking as they did, was their understanding of human biology. This understanding was such as to
make procreation the essential (and only possible moral) intention of sexual activity, and it also goes a long way towards ex-
plaining why the Levitical condemnation of homosexuality is
applied only to men and fails to mention female homosexuality
at all! In the supplement to *The Interpreter's Dictionary of the Bible*
(Nashville, Abingdon Press, 1976), M.H. Pope writes:

> Lack of concern about female homosexuality, in contrast to
> the serious view taken of such activity among males, was
> doubtless due in large measure to belief in the sanctity of
> semen. Without understanding of ovulation and the female
> role in conception, the ancients supposed that the semen sup-
> plied the essential material which coagulated with menstrual
> fluid to produce the embryo or foetus. The woman's part was
> to serve as receptacle and incubator ... Human semen was re-
> garded as almost a person ... and should not be profaned,
> misused, wasted or lost.

To this Professor Biggar adds: 'The rightful, God-given purpose of semen [to the ancients] is to procreate children. Therefore any sexual act that does not intend procreation – such as *coitus interruptus*, masturbation, and any kind of homosexual practice – is morally wrong.'

Given the premise of the argument, to which we shall return shortly, the logic is faultless, and both non-procreative heterosexual sex and homosexuality are neatly ruled out of court. To this 'biological morality' was also added a further major factor which we might call a 'social and political morality'. Thus for much of its history the Jewish race was at war with one or other of its neighbours and, being a relatively small nation when compared with some of the surrounding empires, it was frequently under direct threat as far as its survival was concerned. There was a constant need for a supply of young men to be the nation's warriors and of young women to continue to breed the successive generations. Even in defeat and exile there was an imperative, reinforced by the prophets and especially Jeremiah and Ezekiel, not to despair and dwindle but to grow again and re-populate the nation such that it might one day be restored to its lands and sovereignty. Existing in precarious circumstances for survival such as these, it is again easy to see why the Israelite scriptures should have placed such an emphasis on procreation as essential to sexual activity. And it is easy to see also why any suspicion of homosexual activity could come to be construed as immoral, not only biologically but also socially as putting the very future of Israel at risk by its refusal to adhere to the requirement of procreation. Indeed, further credence is given to the existence of this socio-politically driven form of morality by the fact that it is still operative today. Again, Nigel Biggar is astute in his argument and deserving of substantial quotation:

> The precariousness of social survival, however, is not limited to these [the ancient Israelite] exotic conditions. Up until very recent times it has been universal; infant mortality has been high, adults have died young, and populations have been regularly decimated by waves of war and disease. Under normal conditions in most parts of the world for most of

human history, the task of replenishing the social stock has been an urgent and important one – urgent and important enough to constitute a moral duty. And in many parts of the world even today that is still the case. In these conditions, it is easy to see why homosexual practice [and, we might add, any other sexual practice not designed for procreation] should appear to be a threat to social survival, insofar as it is believed capable of distracting sufficient members of society from doing their duty to populate the next generation. It is not a coincidence, I suggest, that some of the strongest opposition to the normalisation of homosexual practice within the Anglican Church has come from AIDS-ravaged, war-torn, famine-stricken Africa.

Taken together, then, it is not hard to see that the biological understanding and the socio-political circumstances of the ancient world, and in particular of the Jewish people, were largely responsible for the formation of this particular requirement of procreation as a factor in sexual ethics. That it should then have come to be seen as a divine command is no great surprise either: the Old Testament is, amongst other things, a massive repository of etiological stories concerning place-names, people's (and nation's) identities and so on, and once having formulated their ethical rules it was only natural that the Jewish people should have looked to God as the 'cause' of them; and having established this it is only one more logical step to envisage God as actually dictating the rules to his people in the first place. Thus a biologically and socio-politically driven ethic is rapidly transmuted into a divinely revealed one binding on all God's people.

Having established how and why the rules came to be written the way they did (and acknowledging that they do indeed state that procreation is the only moral reason for sexual activity), we now come to the second part of the question: are these overt and unambiguous rules still binding on us today – and again I am aware that in posing this question we are at least skirting the fringes of the wider issue of the whole authority of scripture.

The central problem with this debate is the crucial question:

whence does the authority of scripture come? Does scripture have an inviolable authority as coming from God, or does it only have authority insofar as we are willing to grant authority to it? Or is there, perhaps, some other way of expressing its authority without resorting to quite such a stark either/or scenario? It is somewhat like the question posed by Jesus as to the provenance of John's baptism: 'They discussed it among themselves and said, "If we say, 'From heaven', he will ask, 'Then why didn't you believe him?' But if we say, 'From men'...." (They feared the people, for everyone held that John really was a prophet.) So they answered Jesus, "We don't know".' The difference here, however, is that for the sake of the church and of every individual within it, we need to find a way of saying something rather more positive than simply with the chief priests, the teachers of the law and the elders, 'We don't know'.

It is perhaps presumptuous to attempt to short-circuit such a substantial debate, and especially one which has such relevance to the churches at the present time, but it does seem to me that there is a viable way into this puzzle which leads us to what is, I think, a realistic and satisfactory approach to and engagement with scripture. This is to look critically at the shortcomings of both of the alternatives outlined above – which are, in essence, the two most common opposing views of scriptural authority – and then to ask in the light of these shortcomings what other approach there may be which avoids the excesses of both sides.

First, then, it is, I think, axiomatic to the post-modern (and indeed before that to the modern) mind, that scripture cannot simply have an innate, overriding God-given authority which may not be questioned or challenged. We have explored some of the reasons for this earlier, and here it is enough to say that to hold such a view demands a degree of biblical fundamentalism which is no longer a realistic option for us. It requires us to be so completely fundamentalist that we acknowledge the equal authority of all parts of scripture (since according to this view they are all divinely inspired), and this is a position which not even those who would call themselves fundamentalists actually adhere to in practice. Further than this, though, and regardless of how individual Christians may view the bible, it is patently obvious that pragmatically speaking, scripture exercises no authority whatsoever over the lives of vast numbers of people. Thus even if we wish to claim that scripture has some sort of intrinsic authority, this obviously needs to be complemented by our response to it which acknowledges that authority and is therefore able presumably to exercise judgement as to in what precisely that authority consists. At the very least then we can say that scripture is not an authority 'over against' us, to which we are simply subject willy-nilly, but an authority with which we are profoundly in dialogue as to the exact nature and scope of that authority.

If fundamentalism is one untenable extreme, then the other extreme of what we might call 'ultra-criticalism' is equally untenable and equally dangerous. It begins from the above idea that scripture cannot have any innate overriding (and overall) authority, and extrapolates from this the seemingly logical notion that therefore it must be that we accord authority to scripture insofar as it seems to us to merit it. If outright fundamentalism is dangerous because it puts scripture over and against us, this way is equally dangerous because it puts us over and against scripture. Neither way brings us into creative dialogue with scripture. If fundamentalism pays only lip service to the concepts of human judgement and interpretation, then this approach pays only lip service to the authority of scripture, for ironically, if we decide which pieces of scripture are to have authority then it is in fact we who have authority over scripture and not scripture over us!

There is, however, I believe, another alternative which does bring us into a real dialogue with scripture and which acknowledges fully the ideas both of scriptural authority and of human interpretation and judgement. This alternative, unlike the others, which tend to view scripture as monolithic, appeals to the rich diversity of the bible and to its multiplicity of witnesses to the ways of God.

Rather than a single authority, then, scripture has, as various commentators and biblical scholars have noted, among them most recently Luke Timothy Johnson in his distinguished collection of essays, *The Living Gospel*, a wide variety of *auctoritates*. These may be divergent or even sometimes conflicting, and all of them (individually and corporately), whilst they reflect something of the voice and authority of God, nevertheless reflect that voice and authority as mediated, understood and interpreted through the medium of human intellect and experience with the result that this human understanding may, in equal measure sometimes illuminate and sometimes obscure the divine voice.

This understanding of scripture profoundly affects our understanding of our own task in response to it, a task which now is neither simply to submit to it nor to place ourselves above it. In contrast to both of these alternatives, our task is to attempt to understand the processes of intellect and experience which, in dialogue with God, created the scriptures, and then to ascertain as best we may, by applying our own intellect and experience to the witness of scripture, how much this witness faithfully reflects the nature and authority of God and how much of it is human interpretation (or even misinterpretation), and therefore how we respond to this witness of scripture today.

At first sight this may seem like casuistry, as if we are drawing an all-too-subtle distinction, but it should be firmly emphasised that this process of attempting to understand how scripture came to be written, and to engage in dialogue with its understandings, is nowhere near the same thing as simply sitting in judgement upon it from some supposed exterior critical standpoint. The whole purpose is not to judge scripture but to allow it to speak to us on its own terms so that our intellect and experience engage with that of scripture and tradition in an attempt to meet with the God who is witnessed to there, and to discern how faithful (or sometimes mistaken) that witness to God is, and therefore how we should respond to it today.

In the light of all this, then, what of the present case? In brief, we have followed the above process and are now empowered to

think creatively about our sexuality as a result of the conclusions
of our engagement with scripture. For in the course of this chapter we have explored in some depth the intellect and experience
(biological and socio-political) of those who formulated the biblical rules on non-procreative sex and homosexuality, and, in
understanding how and why those rules came to be formulated,
we have questioned the divine authority of those rules by revealing what was formerly thought to be divine speech and
sanction as being a process of simple etiology. The rules themselves are now seen to be actually very human rules stemming,
quite understandably, from very specific intellectual perceptions and circumstances. We may therefore suggest that as such
they are not binding on us today in very different circumstances
and with very different intellectual perceptions, and that the
church may, without being false to God (or to scripture), move
on from these rules and learn to formulate others which reflect
our ongoing experience, understanding of and engagement
with God.

Thus there is a definite case for the church changing its mind
on this, as on other issues. Clearly procreation is one function
(and, it must be admitted, a major one) of sexual activity, but we
are no longer constrained to see it as the sole defining legitimate
one. Thus the argument which we initiated earlier in this book,
in the context of the problems with metaphysics and inflexibility,
may now be seen to be converging with the results of our exploration of the witness and authority of scripture. From both starting points we are reaching a similar conclusion: namely, that the
old negativity with regard to embodiment and sexuality is no
longer appropriate since it is not, as it was long held to be, irrev-
ocably divinely sanctioned. On the contrary, we may now legitimately begin to argue that our appreciation of, and indeed enjoyment of our bodies in sensuality and sexuality is a potential
moral good and can even be integrated positively with holiness.

In such a changed context, in which the divine qualities of
love and creativity (rather than a set of divinely dictated rules)
form the matrix for our moral being, and in which sexuality is

understood as having to do with far more than simply procreation, but rather with reaching out, giving, going beyond ourselves and so on (as well as with the giving and receiving of pleasure), we can then legitimately begin to argue, almost for the first time, for the equality of heterosexual and homosexual loving.

The implications of doing this are enormous, for it means that we have to listen with a new and attentive ear to the homosexual experience of love, grace and holiness. This is both a challenge and an opportunity, the significance of which Luke Timothy Johnson puts particularly well:

... witness is what the church now needs from homosexual Christians. Are homosexuality and holiness of life compatible? Is homosexual covenantal love according to 'the mind of Christ', an authentic realisation of that Christian identity authored by the Holy Spirit, and therefore 'authored' as well by the scripture despite the 'authorities' speaking against it? The church can discern this only on the basis of faithful witness. The burden of proof required to overturn scriptural precedents is heavy, but it is a burden that has been borne before. The church cannot, should not, define itself in response to political pressure or popularity polls. But it is called to discern the work of God in human lives and adapt its self-understanding in response to the work of God. Inclusivity must follow from evidence of holiness; are there narratives of homosexual holiness to which we must begin to listen?
(Luke Timothy Johnson, *The Living Gospel*, London and New York, Continuum, 2004, p. 65)

If this is right, then not only our metaphysics and our engagement with scripture but also our ethics are seen to be converging towards the same point (which again we have visited previously) at which 'right' and 'wrong' as *a priori* concepts are not a good starting point for sexual, and perhaps any, ethics, and where we may come to learn that ideas of morality might have more to do with love and creativity than with the inflexible application of supposed moral laws to particular activities. 'Right' and 'wrong' may come to be seen as terms which we apply only when we have seen and evaluated the effects of actions, rather than categories by which we can pre-judge actions. And somewhere, to return to where we began this chapter, we need to keep in touch with the God-given joy of our own human (and therefore sexual) embodiment. It is to this and its place in the fullness of our response to God that we must next turn before we can eventually consider issues pertaining first to the church and then to the Kingdom of God, the building up of which is, of course, the ultimate goal of all of our loving.

CHAPTER NINE

The Double Direction of Love

In the course of this study we have approached the subject of ethics from a number of different standpoints: metaphysics, doctrine (and especially our doctrine of God), holiness, and biblical authority. It is time now to begin to draw these various threads together and to present a case for a Christian sexual ethics which sees our sexuality as being integrated with our Christian pilgrimage and our yearning for God, rather than at best separate from it and at worst inimical to it.

As we have explored aspects of ethics from these various standpoints one common factor has, I think, emerged, which is that there is, without playing false to our traditions but nonetheless re-interpreting them substantially, a tremendous potential for a radical new openness towards the basic fact of our state of embodiment and towards many manifestations of our human loving. The intention of this chapter is to integrate this new attitude towards sexuality with our love of God, and to explore why and how it is that our human loving (including overtly sexual loving) may be charged with meaning in this context and not merely in a purely human context.

Doing this will bring us spiral-fashion to rejoin at a higher point in the argument ideas which we have touched upon in previous chapters, and especially the idea that our sexuality may be part of our way to holiness and to genuine spiritual fulfilment. That this can be so has been asserted already: here I propose to delineate more fully how and why this can actually happen. Again we have already alluded to the biblical material (especially the *Song of Songs*) and the language of the mystics which dares to speak of loving God in the language of erotic love, so it is important to remember that even though we may here be developing these ideas further than such writers might have envisaged, the concept of applying ideas of human sexual love to our love of God is not a new one and we are not alone, even within the largely body-negative Christian tradition. It must be admitted, however, that the ideas expressed here are a far cry from the rather grim Augustine-driven ideas of the body weighing down the spirit: what we are exploring here is the exact opposite, namely that the body may actually be at one with the spirit's quest and a means of furthering that quest; that it may not be a ball-and-chain to the spirit, but rather a source of insight and inspiration.

First, though, before we can proceed to consider how our sexual loving might contribute to our spiritual pilgrimage, we need to establish very firmly the absolute interrelatedness of our love for one another (of any variety) and our love for God, for if human love in general is not intimately connected with our love of God then we cannot reasonably expect our erotic loving to be so connected either. No amount of special pleading would then be able to achieve the impossible!

In many ways it seems absurdly obvious and almost a truism that these two kinds of love are closely linked, and yet at another level the message seems somehow not to have got through to large portions of the human race who manage to keep them very successfully in separate compartments. Presidents of the United States of America and Prime Ministers of Great Britain are only the rest of us writ large, and it is astonishing how often Christian faith and love for God can be affirmed and policies then put in place which are patently unloving (and sometimes disastrous) as far as substantial numbers of God's people – who also need loving – are concerned. On a smaller scale, every parish knows how easy it is to 'love' God, and just how difficult it is to love the awkward neighbour or the tide of multi-cultural refugees whose various ethnic identities threaten to overtake our nice main-stream Anglicanism or whatever.

The degree to which the two are successfully divorced and

the vehemence with which the distinction can be maintained was brought home to me very forcibly by an experience which I had something over twenty years ago. I was a theological student on a summer placement in Croydon Parish Church at the time, and one Sunday morning I preached a sermon on precisely this topic – the interrelatedness of our love for one another and our love for God. At the end of the service I was abruptly accosted by a particularly peppery old colonel who said to me: 'Young man, never forget that there is a world of difference between loving God and loving your neighbour.' I was too young and too inexperienced then to raise any objection, but I thought he was wrong then and I still think he is wrong now!

That the colonel (who may of course by now be regretting, like the rich man in the parable, his failure to love the Lazaruses of this world while claiming to love God!) was wrong and that the two are indeed richly connected, is powerfully attested to in scripture. It is a thread which runs right through both the Old and New Testaments. In the Old Testament there is probably no clearer illustration of this than the familiar verse from the prophet Micah (6:8): 'He has showed you, O man, what is good. And what does the Lord require of you? To act justly and to love mercy and to walk humbly with your God.' The implication is clear: walking humbly with God is not complete without paying regard to the needs of one's neighbour, and the two activities are plainly complementary. Similarly one could cite any number of passages from the prophets (especially Amos, Micah and Isaiah) in which the people of Israel are exhorted to pay attention to matters of social justice or mercy rather than to endless prayers and sacrifices in a ritual religion which is divorced from righteous living. In a very real sense, showing love for your neighbour (or at least showing justice and mercy and treating your neighbour properly) is showing one's love for God: love of God is, as it were, 'cashed out' in one's treatment of one's neighbour.

Neither is the New Testament any less outspoken than the Old Testament. There are perhaps at least three different ways in which Jesus reminds his hearers of the close relationship between loving one another and loving God. First and foremost there is the re-stating of the two great commandments (actually the passage on which I preached the sermon mentioned earlier!): 'You shall love the Lord your God with all your heart and with all your soul and with all your mind. This is the first and great commandment. And the second is like it. You shall love your neighbour as yourself.' In fact, of course, these commandments span both testaments, the first commandment having its origin in Deuteronomy and the second in Leviticus, and here they are, in the gospels, re-stated and brought together into a unity.

Secondly, there is the parallelism with regard to forgiveness in the Lord's Prayer. Admittedly this does not mention love as such, but it does link our forgiving of other people with our receiving of forgiveness from God, and forgiving is at least one facet of loving. In the Lord's Prayer our loving forgiveness of others is made the condition for our being forgiven by God: our love for our neighbour (here expressed in forgiveness) is plainly intimately bound up with the flow of love between us and God.

Thirdly there are the parables of Jesus, in which human love is both explored as an active and essential virtue in itself, and again (as in the Lord's Prayer) related to our relationship with God as a factor which directly impinges on that relationship. The parable which, for many people most succinctly encapsulates the essence of love from one human being to another is probably the parable of the Good Samaritan. At one level, the parable appears to be all about human love, and our love for God is nowhere explicitly mentioned, but as well as being almost inexhaustible this parable is also immensely subtle, and I venture to suggest that the relationship between love of God and love of neighbour is powerfully implied even if nowhere overtly stated. Thus it is no accident that the two characters who passed by on the other side should have been a priest and a levite. At one level this indicates merely that they are Jews (and Jews of 'good standing') and serves to differentiate them on a human level from the despised Samaritan who followed on later. At another level, however, it should be remembered that these two were in different ways members of the professional religious class whose lives were overtly devoted (ostensibly at least) to the love of God – in worship, teaching, tithing, religious attendance, meticulous observance of the law and so on. And yet here in the parable it is these two 'God lovers' who fail to love on a human level, and their love of God is exposed as a hollow sham, having no roots in the hard and demanding task of loving God in and through his creation and creatures as well as just spiritually 'in himself'. Indeed, there is an uncanny parallel here with the prophets to whom we have just alluded: neither the priest nor the levite is seen to 'do justice' or 'love mercy' and the whole concept of the humble walk with God is thereby called into radical question. It is, we are left to conclude, the Samaritan who loves not only his neighbour but also God most completely.

Where the Good Samaritan contains this implicit contrast between supposed love of God and genuine love of neighbour, other parables reinforce the connection (established in the Lord's Prayer) between our treatment of one another and the consequent enrichment or rupturing of the relationship between ourselves and God. So, for example, in the parable of the unforgiving servant the relationship between master and servant is ruptured by the servant's failure to remit the debt of his fellow servant. There is no means of truly loving God (and equally of fully receiving God's love) without at the same time truly loving our neighbour. Love of God may be the first of the two Great Commandments, but its realisation is nonetheless entirely contingent upon our fulfilment of the second commandment.

If love of God and love of neighbour are held in this creative tension and parallelism in the parables and teachings of Jesus, then they are no less yoked together in the New Testament epistles. Most obviously there is the epistle of James with its dichotomy between faith and works, but the problem with this epistle is that it is all too often set in opposition to the epistles of St Paul with their emphasis on justification by faith, and either revered or vilified in the comparison. However, James and Paul are in fact nothing more than two sides of the same coin, and each is interested – though from a different viewpoint – in the working-out of both the horizontal and the vertical relationships of love. Thus, for example, one of St Paul's most characteristic methods of writing is to explore some matter of doctrine or to reflect on the meaning of something such as the Incarnation or the resurrection, and then to change tack abruptly and to say, effectively, 'And this is how this relationship should make you live and treat one another.' Our relationship with God is, for St Paul, to inform – and indeed dictate – our way of life and relationships with one another, and conversely, the way we behave (at the deepest levels of love rather than merely the superficial one of courtesy) towards one another is a powerful index of the reality of our faith and our faithfulness to the love which God has revealed to us and which we are pledged in return to offer back to him.

Scripturally, then (and *contra* my peppery colonel), there is ample warrant for the general claim that the depth and practical expression of our love for one another is part and parcel both of our journey toward holiness and of what it means genuinely to love God. And the relationship between the two forms of loving is far more than merely some kind of mechanical 'cause and effect' one: in other words, it is not merely that in loving one another we are, as it were, pushing the right metaphysical buttons to open up the way to God. The relationship is far more organic than that, and is expressive of our need to be open to every avenue of loving if any is to be perfected: in other words, we cannot love perfectly with portions of our mind, heart, will or whatever, but all must be given (which requires both the horizontal and vertical dimensions) if any way of love is to reflect the depth of love of which we are capable.

This requirement to love with all of the means at our disposal was given further layers of meaning for me at the same Glenstal Conference mentioned in the Introduction. My attention was drawn, by Professor William Countryman, to a phrase from one of Thomas Traherne's *Centuries*. It comes from number seventy-two of the First Century: 'God alone cannot be beloved.' The phrase itself is startling, but in its fuller context it is even more revealing:

Wouldst thou love God alone? God alone cannot be beloved. He cannot be loved with a finite love, because He is infinite. Were He beloved alone, His love would be limited. He must be loved in all with an unlimited love, even in all His doings, in all His friends, in all His creatures. Everywhere in all things thou must meet His love. And this the Law of Nature commands. And it is thy glory that thou art fitted for it. His love unto thee is the Law and measure of thine unto Him: His love unto all others the Law and obligation of thine unto all.

These are remarkable words, especially as they come from a writer who in his *The Way to Blessedness* spent page after page elucidating the reasons why we should love God above all things. A startling statement, then, but one which is profoundly true in at least two ways. So what implications might it have for us in the present context?

'God alone cannot be beloved.' This is a prescriptive and challenging statement with no qualifications admitted. Not, 'It is a hard thing to love God alone', but the flat assertion, 'God alone *cannot* be beloved.' Here is encapsulated a straightforward realisation of both our limitations and, conversely and implicitly, our potential as finite embodied beings. What is a limitation in one sense is an opportunity in another.

The central focus of the statement is that we as embodied beings cannot simply love God and God alone – there must be other objects of our love as well as God (and as we have consistently argued, these other loves can indeed become part of our path to loving God more fully also). We cannot love God alone simply because we do not possess the capacity to love purely in the abstract – what might be called a love of pure spirit. We ourselves are not pure spirit, and neither therefore can our love be entirely of this variety. Our love inevitably reflects what we are, and our love is therefore always mediated by our state of embodiment, and therefore it may be argued that we love God most fully in and through our love for others. Our love worked out in our dealings with other human beings is also an offering of love to God.

It may be argued, however, that we do express our love for God more 'directly' than this in, for example, our private prayers and our public worship. At one level this is true, and certainly the focus of such prayer and worship is usually more vertical than horizontal – although, of course, in the church's central act of worship in the Eucharist the horizontal dimension (though sometimes neglected) is vitally important: Eucharist is something we do together and not in private. That said, however, our prayers and our worship are admittedly directed solely towards God. And yet, much though we might sometimes like to ignore the fact, we should not forget that even this 'direct' address to God is mediated through our bodies: in posture, words, actions, movement and the like. Whether we like it or not our love is always embodied, and this returns us to the neighbours around us, even whilst it lifts us also to God.

Equally, though, Traherne's statement speaks volumes about the significance of our love for other people: it is not merely a statement about God; it is a statement about his creation and especially about his creatures. The clear implication of this statement is that our love for God is, in some fashion at least, conditional on or at least dependent upon our love for other objects, and principally our fellow human beings. Our own embodied state is nothing less than a calling to love creation, other human beings and our own selves, and to fail to love creation/others/embodiment is not to love God more but less. I am not criticising asceticism *per se*, but rather that brand of asceticism which becomes a world-denying one, a denial which does not betoken a greater love of God but rather a rejection of the primary means which God has provided for the exercise of our love towards him. And here, having dwelt somewhat on the limitations of our finitude, is the opportunity afforded by Traherne's statement: whilst we may not aspire to a love of pure spirit, nonetheless we are called to love God more and more powerfully in and through the created order and, importantly, even in our most direct prayers, through the medium of our embodiment. Our own body is not a spiritual prison or deadweight, but actually the means through which we may draw near to God.

The corollary of this view (radical in terms of so much of our tradition) is, I suggest, that a fully embodied commitment to loving, and an equally full acceptance of the embodied nature of that love, is therefore essential to our experience of loving God also. Our love of God and therefore (given, as we have seen, that this is worked out and even forged in action among our neighbours) our own holiness demands a full acceptance of and rejoicing in all aspects of human creative loving.

There is, I am acutely aware, one *caveat* to be entered here, and it is one which we have had cause to draw attention to previously. That is, it should not be thought that I am advocating any kind of a return to 'free love' or to an 'anything goes' mentality and morality. There are, and must be, standards and touchstones in our human relationships (sexual and non-sexual) in order to establish what is genuinely loving behaviour and what is merely dressed-up selfishness, power-seeking, domination or exploitation. These standards and touchstones are things such as the creativity, self-offering, vulnerability and mutual enrichment which we have touched on at various points in this study. Without these and similar fruits our actions are at best barren and at worst destructive.

Equally, my emphasis on erotic love should not be interpreted as being a claim that every sexual experience is related to holiness, or that the lack of sexual experience is any kind of hindrance to holiness! Plainly there are very many celibates whose lives are imbued with holiness, and many unloving or destructive sexual activities which mar or detract from our pursuit of holiness. Contrary to such possible misconceptions, it should be plainly stated that what I am arguing is this: that if it is 'given' to us to have the experience of genuinely loving erotically and sexually then this experience, in all its rich fullness of expression and mutuality, may be a part of our overall growth in love and therefore ultimately in holiness. Furthermore it should be noted that this is not a study devoted to any kind of exaltation of sexuality, but more about simply raising it from the abyss to which Christian history has largely consigned it! I am emphatically not arguing that erotic loving is better than or superior to any other forms of human loving, but merely that, contrary to much of the received opinion of negative Christian tradition, neither is it any worse! Sexuality may be (although it by no means always is) part of the way to holiness and love of God just as much as, but no more than, charity.

To conclude this chapter and before we move on to consider some of the implications of this view of sexuality, as far as first loving human beings and secondly the church are concerned, there is perhaps one further point to be made as to why it is that our sexuality may be one way (among many) which can lead us towards God. Thus it appears to be true of all of our loving human relationships that they reinforce one another. All of us play many different and interlinked loving roles with a wide variety of people, and we often learn from one situation and role something (perhaps even many things) which we may profitably bring to an entirely different situation and role. It may be therefore that our experiences of friendship with our peers may help us better to parent our children, perhaps by enabling us to avoid typical parent/child flashpoints (especially in the teenage years) and to slip into another and more constructive role as friend rather than (temporarily, at least) as parent. Similarly, our experience of being mentor, provider or listener to another person may teach us the grace to enable us to receive for ourselves the ministry of someone else in due course.

So too, it may be, I suggest, with our experience of sexual loving. No more than any other variety of loving is it a self-contained category of loving all on its own – although, of course, its expressions are rather more restricted! Nonetheless, our experience of sexual loving may (indeed perhaps should) reciprocate with and inform our other modes of loving. Sexual love, as we have seen, carries its own especial graces of offering, giving, vulnerability, transcendence and openness, among others. None of these may necessarily be unique to sexual love, but they are all particularly obvious and powerful in such a context, and these especial qualities of sexual love may (and hopefully will) go to reinforce and enrich our other experiences of loving (and non-sexual) relationships, including directly and vitally, our love for and relationship with God.

Thus, I suggest, as we approach what will be at once the most radical and the most positive (and to some the most challenging and even threatening) sections of this book, there is scriptural, traditional and experiential warrant for the idea that if we can learn to love our bodies (and with them our sexuality) and rejoice in our full creative humanity, we may in the end be more open both to giving and receiving love from others and from God – and what, it may be asked, is our Christian calling about if it is not about this human and divine exchange of love, begun now in this life and fulfilled in ways we cannot now predict or understand in the mystery of eternal life.

CHAPTER TEN

The Love that Dares to Speak its Name

In one way this chapter is something of an interlude; in another
it is very much at the heart of this book. All of our arguments to
date have concerned various aspects of what it means to be embodied and what this implies both for our human experience of
loving and for our love of God and our growth towards holiness. Given that we are all embodied and all, therefore, constrained (and graced) in the same way, it should, I hope, have
become evident that this is not a proselytising or aggressive 'one
issue' book. Embodiment does affect us all, and I suggest that
we have all (or nearly all) inherited a less-than-helpful legacy
when it comes to evaluating our experience of that embodiment
in love, and especially sexual love, and even more when this is
related to, or even contrasted with, our 'primary' duty of love
for God.

That disclaimer made, however, there is equally an underlying primary issue behind the writing of this book as the introduction made plain, although it is my hope that its central thesis
will be of value to people of all sexual orientations. This primary
issue is that of homosexuality. We have explored the ideas of
non-procreative sex and the need for the touchstones of giving,
self-offering and so on in erotic love, and one hopes that these
ideas will have resonances for heterosexual couples in all sorts
of situations: Roman Catholic couples wrestling with the
Vatican's teaching on contraception; couples who are fearful of,
yet wanting variety in their sexual life; couples (and they do
exist) longing to escape from the prison of feeling that every
time they make love there is something 'wrong' with what they
have done, however nice it feels and however much it enriches

their relationship; and simply the many people who feel ill at ease with their own body, its urges and desires and their longing to be physically close to another human being.

All of this said, it remains true that the genesis of this book at the Glenstal Conference was the pan-Anglican, indeed pan-church debate on homosexuality which is so rife and potentially so divisive at present. (Indeed, this chapter was written in the last few days before the publication of the report of the Lambeth Commission which arose precisely out of the need to explore the maintenance of communion in the light of this very issue and the strong antipathies which it has aroused within the Anglican Communion.) It is, therefore, having laid much of the ground-work, and before concluding with other and wider consider-ations, time to address this specific issue head on. For there is a huge moral question at stake, the resolution of which, one way or the other, has equally huge implications both for the church as a corporate entity and for the many individual homosexuals who desire membership of it. The moral question, though vast, is essentially simple (in formulation, if not in answer): is homo-sexuality straightforwardly wrong, or are we as a church, in maintaining that it is wrong (as by and large officially we do), imposing the most heartless, vicious and un-Christian set of rules on a substantial portion of the human race who only want to love both God and neighbour fully like the (comfortably het-erosexual) rest of us?

Setting aside, very briefly, the underlying ethical issues for a moment, it certainly seems to me that the Anglican Church in particular has, especially since Lambeth 1998, got its handling of this issue both thoroughly muddled and, in fact, fatally ethically compromised. Thus we are currently locked into a homosexual double-speak which is meaningless, confusing and painful. That this is so is hardly surprising given the recent track record of the Church of England especially on 'fudging' crucial issues.

It is not very many years since the issue of the ordination of women was the major one exercising the minds of many Anglican provinces, the Church of England included, and in-

deed exactly the same problems of communion were being de-
bated. For a substantial number of provinces the matter was re-
solved fairly straightforwardly even if often (to some) painfully.
A decision was taken by synod, convocation or whatever and,
effectively, where one day there were not women priests, the
next day there were (or at least could be).

The Church of England, however, handled the whole issue
somewhat differently, and the current danger is that the whole
Anglican Communion is in peril of following its 'mother
church's' lead on this previous issue and applying the same sort
of criteria to the debate on homosexuality – criteria of double-
think and double-speak which ultimately resolve nothing, satisfy
no-one and inflict continuing and deeper pain on at least some
of the parties concerned.

Thus in the case of the ordination of women the double-
speak involved both individuals, parishes and the order of the
church as a whole. Individual dissenting clergy were given, effectively, two options: financial compensation if they felt moved
to resign over the issue (a decision which they had, incidentally,
ten years to make!), or the freedom to move to a similarly-minded
parish which had passed some or all of the infamous resolutions
A, B or C. For parishes, the 'opt-out clause' was the passing of
these same resolutions and applying for the oversight of a
Provincial Episcopal Visitor or 'flying bishop' as they rapidly
came to be known. And so to church order! Historically and
theologically the mere notion of alternative episcopal oversight
is nonsense, and the idea of any diocese having (no matter what
spin may be put on it) two bishops is absurd. Also, in connection
with bishops, the Church of England divorced the ordination of
women to the priesthood from the issue of election to the episcopate, so that at present women, though priests, are not eligible to
become bishops. There is no possible theological justification for
this, and the concept of having two classes of priests, one eligible
for episcopacy and one not is theologically risible and thoroughly
offensive. The double-think is everywhere: we have women
priests (but not here in such and such a parish); we value

women priests (but they mustn't become bishops); we approve of women priests (but not enough to have the courage of our convictions and insist upon them, so we will allow resolutions and Provincial Episcopal Visitors for the 'No's); and so on and so on. And the practical results are leading, and will continue to lead, to indescribable chaos: at this stage several years on, which bishops are 'tainted' by the ordination of women and which are not? Which clergy have been ordained by which bishop? Which parishes are willing to accept whose ministry? And so, while there are double standards employed, it will continue, with the situation becoming ever more complex with the passing of the years until the puzzle (assuming that anyone still cares about it) will be completely insoluble.

That the Church of England should have handled the debate over the ordination of women in this fashion was unfortunate in itself, but an even greater problem is that this double-speak and double-standards approach seems to have set a precedent for the way in which at least the less theologically conservative parts of the Anglican Communion are prepared to handle other major debates, including, pressingly at present, that on homosexuality. (At the other end of the scale, of course, is the implacable opposition to homosexuality exhibited by substantial portions of the African church and spearheaded by such figures as the Archbishop of Nigeria. This position has the merit of honesty, but as we have argued in our consideration of scripture and its authority, has also the demerits of theological naïvete, scriptural literalism and historical ignorance.)

In large measure this latest theological and ecclesiological variation on the Church of England 'fudge' theme appears to have emanated from the resolutions of the 1998 Lambeth Conference. Admittedly one has to have a certain degree of sympathy for the bishops involved, for it is hard to see even now, and let alone several years earlier in the debate, how any genuinely satisfactory resolution of the vast differences of opinion involved could have been achieved. What emerged, though, was not a resolution of the issue one way or the other (even an

interim one), nor even a more or less satisfactory compromise
position but, frankly, a muddle.

Of the various resolutions regarding human sexuality, the
two most pertinent (and most frequently quoted) are those in
paragraphs (c) and (d) which stated that the conference:

(c) recognises that there are among us persons who experience themselves as having a homosexual orientation. Many
of these are members of the church and are seeking the pastoral care, moral direction of the church, and God's trans-
forming power for the living of their lives and the ordering of
relationships. We commit ourselves to listen to the experience of homosexual persons and we wish to assure them that
they are loved by God and that all baptised, believing and
faithful persons, regardless of sexual orientation, are full
members of the Body of Christ;

(d) while rejecting homosexual practice as incompatible with
scripture, calls on all our people to minister pastorally and
sensitively to all, irrespective of sexual orientation, and to
condemn irrational fear of homosexuals, violence within
marriage and any trivialisation and commercialisation of sex.

To these resolutions may be added the further one that the bishops
'cannot advise' the legitimising of same sex unions or the ordination of people involved in a same sex union.

It all sounds plausible enough at a first glance: the bishops
have achieved the impossible task of at once upholding biblical
and traditional standards of Christian marriage, and at the same
time recognised the needs of others for whom this 'standard' is
not appropriate or possible. Underneath these urbane and pol-
ished statements, however, there lies another reality: that of
complete and utter theological and ethical muddleheadedness
and the employment (whether wilfully or ignorantly) of a totally
unacceptable moral double standard.

This stems, it appears, from an unresolved confusion (or
blindness) about the contradictoriness of saying one thing about
the moral status of homosexuality and quite another thing about
our response to it. Thus on the one hand we are, by these resolu-

tions, committed to 'listening' to the experience of homosexuals and assuring them of God's love for them and of their place in the church (aren't we so kind?), and on the other hand we continue firmly to tell this same group that what they do is wrong, that we cannot in any way bless their love, and that although they may have a place in the church their sexual orientation is a bar to priesthood. So, it appears, homosexuals are now to be loved, cherished and accepted although wrong! Pardon me, but you can't have it both ways! Either homosexuality is fully acceptable within the life of the church or it is not. If the experiences of those who are wrong need to be listened to, then why not go a little further and encourage the church to 'listen' to the experiences of child murderers, drug barons and terrorists – or why not be honest and admit that homosexuality is totally compatible with holiness and that these other activities are not! It would not be an easy path for the church to take and it would not be without pain for some – possibly many – any more than a total and complete rejection of homosexuality would. But one day, and probably sooner rather than later, this is a choice which the church is simply going to have to face head on, and in the search for a lasting resolution of the issue, the confusions and ethical dualism of Lambeth 1998 are of no service to anyone, liberal or conservative. There is undoubtedly trauma ahead for the church as the subject is addressed, but eventually the church will need to have the courage of its convictions one way or the other, and either unequivocally embrace those of a homosexual orientation or equally unequivocally exclude them. The present climate of conditional toleration (conditional, among other things, on homosexuals meekly accepting being told that they are wrong) is not, in the end, acceptable: as we heard at Glenstal, 'Don't tolerate us! Either hate us or love us, but don't just tolerate us!'

This book is one attempt to go beyond toleration and to explore the territory where 'Yes' might be said to homosexuality and to see what effects this might have not only for homosexuals but also for heterosexuals and for the life – and ecclesiological identity – of the church.

In the course of this attempt various ideas – scriptural, doctrinal and ethical – have emerged which might enable us as a
church to change our perspective and our thinking on homosexuality, or at least move the debate a little further on, and before
we consider what a 'Yes' saying church might begin to look like,
it is important that we should highlight, even briefly, these various pointers toward change.

First, then, the position with regard to scripture is nowhere
near as clear cut as theological conservatism would have us believe. The bible is the product of (and the possessor of) not one
but many *auctoritates*, and its condemnation of homosexuality
(by a very small percentage of those *auctoritates*) can profitably
be explained by an examination of the cultural pre-occupations
of the societies which framed that condemnation. Beyond this,
scripture demands that we engage with it (rather than either
meekly submit to it or arrogantly judge it or ignore it), and that
we seek, in dialogue with both scripture and experience, to discern more clearly the nature of the God who stands behind and
within scripture and to fashion our lives both doctrinally and
ethically in the light, not of the letter of scripture, but of this dis-
cernment resulting from engagement with it. Thus we have argued in previous chapters that scripture cannot be naïvely 'quarried' for proof-texts, and that more important than particular cul-
turally-derived rules is the witness of scripture to the nature and
qualities of God and most especially the key qualities of creativity
and love.

Secondly, in terms of doctrine and ethics, we have argued for
a thoroughgoing review of our metaphysical presuppositions
and for an appreciation of both God and ethics which is more
flexible and creative than many of our traditional categories of
thought readily allow for. Specifically we have inferred from
this that *a priori* conceptions of morality are no longer justifiable
either scripturally or doctrinally: that 'right' and 'wrong' are
secondary concepts, the validity of which depends upon other
primary concepts (notably again creativity and love), and that
we can no longer argue for any system of ethics simply on the

(entirely circular) grounds that 'God says so' or 'the bible says so'. There needs to be a reason for our ethics, not merely a putative divine fiat.

Thirdly, and turning particularly to the realm of human sexuality, we have, as well as undoing the negative aspects of the Christian approach to it, also attempted directly to foster a more positive approach. Embodiment, though a limited state, is a graced one and not an imprisoning or downgrading one, and it is properly related both to love and holiness. In turn this has led us to contend that procreation is not the sole legitimate reason for sexual activity, and that the reciprocal giving and receiving of love, affirmation (and joy) is of the essence of all human sexual loving – and there is no reason why this should not include homosexual as well as heterosexual loving.

That said, there are, as we have already seen, criteria for sexual (as for any other) loving, and we are looking here not to validate any and every form of sexual relationship, but rather those which manifest the qualities of self-giving, vulnerability, self-transcendence and so on which we have explored earlier. Similarly, it should be stressed that this book is not an *apologia* for all homosexual activity regardless of ethical value. It is taken as read that within homosexual relationships the same obligations of fidelity and mutual self-giving apply as in heterosexual relationships. And here, on a purely practical level, it should be noted that it is precisely acceptance and affirmation which will most probably encourage those standards to flourish. Thus one of the (spurious) arguments against accepting homosexuality is the supposed permissiveness, predatoriness and promiscuity of a homosexual lifestyle. To this accusation three rejoinders should, I think, be made.

The first of these is that quite simply their (exclusively heterosexual) accusers do not have a leg to stand on! Over one third of marriages end in divorce, increasing numbers of people marry two, three or even four times (hence the development of the interesting concept of 'serial polygamy'), many choose not to marry at all but to cohabit with varying levels of commitment, and I forget what the average number of sexual partners in a lifetime is supposed to be, but I do remember thinking when I read the figures that I was several dozen in arrears by my fortieth birthday! We either need to re-think our attitudes to human sexual loving radically altogether, or return to a blanket 'they are all wrong' mentality. What we cannot do is to single out one group and use them as the scapegoat for the general practice of society. Yes, some homosexuals I am sure may be promiscuous, but they would appear not to be entirely alone in this!

The second rejoinder is the equally obvious fact that many homosexuals are not promiscuous, but live for many years in exclusive relationships of great love and tenderness with a single partner, and their witness to an ethical way of homosexual loving should not be obscured or downgraded. My own consciousness of this has recently been rekindled by reading a book written by a parishioner of mine. Gerard Bourke has recently written *Out on a Limb* – also interesting sub-titled *The King of Love my Shepherd is* (Victoria, Canada, Trafford Publishing, 2003), and there can be no doubting the sincerity of Gerard's love for George nor the grief which comes through powerfully at George's death, or the sense of new life injected by his more recent love for Na. Reading it one cannot feel that this is a record of human sexual sin, but a testament to our human ability to love – and this, regardless of sexual orientation, is surely of ethical value.

Thirdly, then, if this faithfulness and devotion is the touchstone of authentic homosexual as of heterosexual loving, is it not the case that full acceptance and affirmation of such love will lead to the furthering of such ethical standards. It is hardly surprising, given its history, that homosexual loving has not always been of this devoted and faithful kind. It would be an interesting experiment to see what would happen to the pattern of heterosexual relationships if, for say, a trial period of two hundred years, marriage were to be outlawed and any overt commitment prohibited on pain of imprisonment! Given the right climate one might expect the values of genuine love and fidelity to flourish more rather than less readily within the (substantial) homosexual community. Gerard's story is not unique even during the years of social opprobrium and, in some places, criminality, but for many the full empowerment to love creatively and faithfully will only come as a consequence of the acceptance of the nature of that love rather than its condemnation.

These various practical – rather than purely doctrinal or metaphysical – considerations lead to the final reflection of this chapter, in the light of which we may then proceed to other wider matters such as ecclesiological implications. This is simply the need for openness towards each other and towards the future. The point was particularly well made by Victor Griffin (the retired Dean of St Patrick's National Cathedral, Dublin) in a recent Catalyst pamphlet and deserves substantial quotation here:

> We are made in the image of God the Creator, and therefore we too are creators as well as creatures. God expects us to use our freedom and initiative to seek, explore, experiment, indeed to take risks, to proceed by trial and error; in a word to use our intellects. We are bidden 'to love God with all our mind' which means always to keep an open and receptive mind to contemporary knowledge and experience when seeking an answer to complex questions.
>
> Absolutism, the conviction that we have 'the truth, the whole truth and nothing but the truth', is the product of a closed mind, stemming from fear of the unknown, addicted to certainty and finality when confronted with complexity. When absolutists are in control, others must pay the price, often a terrible price in suffering. Pascal said: 'Men never do evil so completely and cheerfully as when they do it for religious conviction.' We might also add 'from a political or racist conviction'. History, not least in the 20th century, is a witness to this shameful fact.
>
> The truth is that we live in a imperfect world. Utopia is always out of our reach, and we can only strive to achieve that which is the least imperfect in an imperfect world. 'Knowing

only in part and seeing through a mirror darkly' as St Paul puts it should teach us humility before God and respect and tolerance towards our fellowmen. Absolutism is the refuge of the closed mind imprisoned in a tomb which never opens to release a resurrection.

In 'the changes and chances of this fleeting world' what we can and must do is to strive to maximise mutual respect and tolerance and minimise suffering, and leave the rest to God. In this way we shall endeavour to love God and our neighbour.

(*Christian and Homosexual? Anglicans Consider the Issues*, Catalyst Pamphlet No. 11, Belfast 2004, Christianity and Homosexuality, pp.8-20 (p.19).

To this I would only add the need for the wisdom of Gamaliel and the truth that 'by their fruits you will know them'. Before us lies a period of waiting, whilst accepting and loving and nurturing the whole church, homosexual and heterosexual, as we attempt to discern the movement of God's Spirit in the world today. There may be some who wish simply to reject and exclude, and it would undoubtedly be simpler (though not, I think, easier or less painful) to do so: but can we afford not to attempt to extend the church and God's Kingdom to all and, ultimately, do we have any right whatsoever not to do so, but rather precisely the obligation to reach out in God's name to all?

CHAPTER ELEVEN

A Church for All

Thus far our discussion of sexuality has led us in and out of a wide variety of disciplines, of which ethics has been but one. Our understanding of sexuality and our evaluation of it in ethical terms have been seen to be dependent upon our previous exploration of a number of other areas such as the nature of God, the authority of scripture and the uses and limits of metaphysical thought. That these links between apparently very different areas of thought should exist is hardly surprising, for theology is a realm which not only encompasses a range of subject areas (such as doctrine, history and biblical studies) but one which also borders on, and interrelates with what are, strictly speaking, other disciplines entirely, such as philosophy and ethics. The whole theological endeavour is, if you like, somewhat akin to an intellectual and spiritual version of the children's game of 'pick-up sticks': it is very hard indeed to move one part of the heap without disturbing other portions of it, which may appear to be some distance away but which are actually very firmly connected.

In terms of our present discussion, this web of inter-relations between different thought areas has meant that as well as ranging through quite a number of them along the way, there has been yet one more hovering somewhere in the background – to which we have very briefly alluded from time to time – and demanding at some point to make a proper entrance. This hitherto shadowy companion is ecclesiology, and it is at this point essential to address it, although we shall do so from a very different standpoint from the Windsor Report. For the most part we have to date been concerned to explore the doctrinal and ethical principles which should inform our thinking on sexuality and to look at what effects these might have on the lives of individuals, but clearly there are also implications in all of this for the church – for its own self-understanding and sense of identity – and it is these implications to which we must now turn.

The primary ecclesiological consideration to which our reflections have led us is not so much the question 'What is the church?' as the question 'Who is the church?' Throughout its history and in, I suspect, almost every one of its denominational forms, the church has had a ready answer to this question. The church (or at least such and such a denominational branch of it) is composed of those who subscribe to a particular confessional formula or who have been baptised and confirmed or who adhere to an approved spiritual and/or moral code. By the same token, those who do not fulfil whatever the criteria may be are, effectively, excluded. Thus, for example, the Presbyterian Church has had the Westminster Confession as its touchstone of orthodoxy, and the Roman Catholic Church has outlawed those (such as the Modernists in a past age, or more recently Hans Kung and others) who transgressed doctrinally, and has disciplined those (such as divorcees and couples practising artificial contraception) who have stepped outside the official limits of that church's moral teaching. The tests and criteria for membership may vary between traditions, but each has in its own way always enjoyed at least something of the security of Cyprian's 'ark of salvation' metaphor and had the comforting feeling that whatever spiritual deluge may imperil others they at least are safely afloat, whether in the barque of St Peter, the heavy cruiser of Calvinism, or the slightly leaky tramp steamer of Anglicanism!

Such a model of membership and fixed identity is, however, fast losing credibility today, a process which will be radically accelerated if ideas such as those in this book begin to gain currency. Thus the church's identity (even if not as yet its own articulation of that identity) is changing already in response to a changing society. People are more mobile today than they have ever been before – geographically, politically, economically, employment-wise, holiday-wise and so on – and this is reflected in a corresponding sense of spiritual mobility. Yes, of course there are still many people who are born and brought up in one church and remain there for their entire lifetime, but ever-increasing numbers of people are exploring different patterns and traditions from those in which they were raised – if, indeed, they were raised in any at all.

I am, for example, acutely aware of this in my own parochial ministry. In one rural Irish Anglican parish we have several cradle Roman Catholics, one of whom is even exploring the possibility of Anglican priesthood, a wide variety of continental European 'Protestants' of varying hues, and a substantial population of 'honorary' parishioners who, whilst remaining in principle Roman Catholics are just as likely to worship in the Anglican Cathedral as in the Roman Catholic Parish Church, and equally likely to choose to receive communion in the one as in the other. Similarly we have parishioners – and some very faithful ones – who, if they go away on holiday to an area with a wider variety of church options than is available here, would naturally gravitate perhaps to a Baptist church or a Presbyterian church rather than to another Church of Ireland parish.

In all directions the edges of church membership are blurring, and this will one day – and hopefully the sooner the better – need to be reflected in each individual church's perception of itself and its identity *vis-à-vis* the overall concept of 'church'. Into this increasingly fluid, fluctuating and shifting pattern of response to the question 'Who is the church?' the ideas expressed in this book flow very naturally, for it is a pattern which can at last begin to define itself inclusively rather than exclusively. For too long the church has kept at arm's length those who do not conform to the supposed ethically acceptable norms of sexuality – in other words those who are neither single and celibate or in a life-long (first) marriage. Cohabitees, divorcees (especially remarried ones) and homosexuals have been expected to appear in church – if allowed to appear at all – as repentant sinners rather than as rejoicing and thankful members of the people of God and the household of faith. In recent years the attitude has admittedly changed substantially with regard to cohabitees and divorcees but not, officially at least, with regard to homosexuals. There are, undoubtedly, many parishes and congregations which welcome homosexuals warmly, but there still lurks in the background even of these parishes, the spectre of 'official' disapproval. Even the resolutions of the 1998 Lambeth Conference make it very plain, in spite of their eirenic tone of 'listening', that homosexuality is still officially frowned upon and that practising Christianity and practising homosexuality are, at a point somewhere just beyond the reach of the measured and meaningless language of the resolutions, fundamentally incompatible if not mutually exclusive.

What I am advocating here is a radically different perception of 'church': one in which all of our double-speak with regard to sexuality and especially homosexuality is removed, and in which our sexuality may be evaluated and understood in some of the positive ways which we have explored in this book. Such a church would learn to acknowledge and celebrate the richness of human sexuality and would learn to see it as integrated with the rest of our humanity, including our journey towards holiness, and not as an isolated and largely negative part of our human make-up. It would learn also to apply criteria such as those of creativity and self-giving in its evaluation of sexuality, and would learn to find these qualities in all genuine human loving (sexual and otherwise) both between the sexes and within them. Finally, it would learn to recognise the grace of Christ-like and Christ-inspired love in all faithful Christian living and loving, regardless of sexual orientation.

The effect of such a church (as well as its own sense of identity) would be profoundly different from that which has obtained in the past and is still all too much with us in the present. From being a church which (in all of its denominational forms) has been for a substantial minority of the human race, marginalising, shaming and excluding, it might (and I would argue should) move to being a church which is precisely the opposite of this: demarginalising and de-shaming, a church which is a powerful witness to the healing and integrating power of a loving God and not to the pain and guilt-inflicting power of an often judgemental and cruel humanity. The church should be a place and a people to which all are welcome as equals and as fellow pilgrims, regardless of sexual orientation, and in which we can see further than a set of supposed rules of dubious origin and towards the heart of God's loving and creative purpose for, and relationship with humanity. In this vision is a church which might then meet the Glenstal plea for love rather than toleration.

Having said earlier in this chapter that this question of 'Who is the church?' is the primary one to which we have been led here, it is equally important to indicate that this is by no means the only ecclesiological issue which is outstanding at the present time. Indeed, it is an issue which is part of what will prove to be quite possibly the greatest shift in the church's self-understanding for several hundred years – the question of not simply 'Who is the church?' but of 'What is the fundamental nature of that church of which these people are a part?'

This is, to put it mildly, a huge topic, and it is one which I propose to explore more thoroughly in another book, since it has its roots not only in the issues we have discussed here but in an array of other topics (themselves large enough for books), such as the place of *agnosis* in faith and the rigorous employment of the *via negativa* as the foundation of all theological method. However, as its ramifications also concern us here it is important to visit the subject, even if not in any great detail.

The church's fundamental self-understanding is usually best expressed – as Avery Dulles successfully demonstrated some twenty-odd years ago – by the use of models. My models are somewhat different from Dulles' and there are fewer of them, and they are designed to illustrate not so much what the church is 'doing' or seeking to show forth, but more what the church feels itself to be 'in its own bones' so to speak.

Traditionally, then, the church has been largely what I have

come to call a 'dispensing church'. That this is and has been the
case is reflected in much of the language which we use to describe the individual's relationship with that church. Where the
church dispenses the individual naturally enough receives, and
so we speak, for example, of receiving communion, receiving
absolution and receiving a blessing. The reality of this dispensing church goes far deeper, however, than merely these external
manifestations of things given by the church and received by the
individual. The metaphor of the church as dispenser has
reached right to the heart of the individual's relationship with
the church, such that the church has been seen – at least as much
as God – as the dispenser or withholder of grace and even of salvation. Keep the rules and remain in favour with the church and
all will be well: step outside these church-sanctioned boundaries
and salvation itself is in jeopardy.

In matters of faith the church has understood itself to hold all
the answers, and the individual's task is simply to 'buy into' this
package of faith. In doing so the believer gains knowledge (mediated through the church) of God's will, rules, nature and so on,
and is told precisely what must be believed and done in order to
comply with God's demands in both faith and practice. There is
little need to think and even less to question: just believe and behave and the church, through its dispensing of grace and salvation, will take care of the rest.

If this model of a dispensing church is on the decline, as I believe it is, then the model which most accurately characterises its
replacement – that is, the church which is slowly and falteringly
evolving into being at the present time – is that of the 'seeking'
church. The concept of a seeking church is one which identifies
the individual with the church far more closely than the dispensing model does. In the dispensing model, the church (in its
institutions, hierarchies, formulae etc) is set over against the individual: in a seeking church both the church as corporate body
and the individual within it are seen to be involved in the same
activities and share the same priorities. Such a church is one
which has relinquished its hold upon the spurious absolutes and

inflexible rules of a previous age, and has recognised in practice and in preaching – as it has long since done in theory – the practical, conditional and provisional nature of all of our beliefs and 'knowledge' of God's nature and demands upon us. In recognising this, the church will be able to see itself much more in practice – as again it does in theory – as a people *in via*, a pilgrim church which is, by nature, always seeking corporately and individually for ever further glimpses of that ultimate mystery which is God. As such, and as avowedly a seeking church which does not claim to possess all knowledge and all answers, it will be a church which is, vitally, ever open to new insights and to finding new riches concerning the things of God in the experiences of all of its members.

If the church can – as I believe it must – come to see itself in this light, then this in turn will have enormous potential consequences for the ways in which it views its common life and the opinions (and indeed practices) of its individual members. A church which believes that it possesses all of the answers has a fundamentally different outlook and polity from one which is acutely aware that it does not. Thus we have argued here for the theological (and hence the ecclesiological) impossibility of any kind of an all-knowing and therefore 'dispensing' church. We have seen that we cannot 'know' a definitive set of rules from God, and that ethics needs to be thought and prayed into via a rigorous exploration of the relevant areas of doctrine.

In terms of ecclesiology, this leads naturally to a church which is aware of the partial nature of its knowledge and aware also of its own ongoing journey towards both faith and holiness. And this sense of 'incompleteness' and ongoing pilgrimage (with its consequent lack of closure) should have profound consequences for the church's ability to live with and learn from difference and diversity. A church which 'knows' has a closed mind, but a church which seeks has, potentially at least, an open mind – open to where that seeking might lead it, and open to the exploration of possibilities, some of which may turn out to be blind alleys or false turnings, and aware also that exploring these avenues is the only means of establishing which of them will prove ultimately fruitful and which will not.

At present then, certainly within Anglicanism, and probably equally so in all denominations, we have a church which is finding it increasingly hard to live positively in the face of diversity and difference, and I would argue that this is in large measure due to its perception of itself as a church which, on the whole, 'knows' and dispenses. Somewhere in the background, in the shadows of this church, a new identity is slowly gestating, which for the sake of the whole church must one day be brought to birth: a church which knows its own provisionality and the provisionality of all of its pronouncements and beliefs, and which is therefore capable of learning to live with diversity and difference (and disagreement) whilst attempting corporately to discern what behaviours do seem to be genuinely creative and loving.

This perception has recently been beautifully articulated by the Bishop of Newcastle (Australia), Roger Herft, in the *Journal of Anglican Studies*. Interestingly, he relates his comments to the work of the Lambeth Commission, whose 'unenviable task', he says, was to create a 'road map' for the Anglican Communion. In common with the thoughts expressed here, Herft casts doubt on the viability of such a 'road map' with its overtones of precision and closure. Instead he invokes the image of travellers conversing with one another (a little in the manner of Chaucer's pilgrims sharing stories) as being the way forward. He concludes, using much the same language as we have independently employed here:

> The Anglican Communion, with its claim to 'provisional identity' in the divine scheme of salvation, may be called to engage in a process that enables travellers to converse rather than to become absorbed in the task of drawing a definite road map. We may find that in that conversation is the ground to conversion, to holiness, to being made whole ourselves and to offer hope to the anonymous ones of the world.
> *Journal of Anglican Studies*, Volume 2.1, June 2004, pp. 96-98, (p.98).

As it draws to a close, that is very much the hope with which this book is written: that it might be part of a conversation and indeed a conversion in which we might be able to see ourselves differently as church, in such a way that we are open to new forms and experiences of holiness, and to see ourselves as a 'seeking' church which is, by definition, open to all who would seek, and from each of whom we might learn a little more of what it means to be human, to be holy, to be embodied and sexual beings, and to be creative and loving in fidelity to the (admittedly mysterious) nature of our creative and loving God. Whether we can become such a church is another matter and a different story. For the present we can only hope and pray.

CONCLUSION

A Funny Thing Happened
on the Way to the Kingdom

Theologically speaking the church is an earnest of – indeed a
sacrament of –the Kingdom of God. It at once is, and is not that
Kingdom; it is related to it and embodies it and yet it is not the
fullness of it. In the church the Kingdom of God is both here and
not yet. At one level the church is part of that Kingdom, and yet
at another level it simply prefigures what will be.

The identification between church and Kingdom may not be
complete, but there is enough of a connection between them to
indicate that the church should at least encapsulate and incarn-
ate, as far as is humanly possible, some of the values of that
Kingdom (which, incidentally, often overturn our own most
cherished and longest held convictions) if it is convincingly to
bear witness to it and exist as a foretaste of it. This requirement
in turn has two implications for the church as a Kingdom community, in terms of the issues raised in this book.

First, then, we have argued here for the loving and creative
nature of God and for the view that our own embodied and sexual being reflects in all of its genuine loving (heterosexual and
homosexual) this prior nature of God. If this is so, it is unthinkable that God should exclude from his Kingdom any whose
lives are thus loving and creative, whatever their sexual orientation. Similarly, if morality has more to do with doctrine and
holiness than with a set of *a priori* rules about specific activities,
then the touchstone of morality is not activities *per se* but the attitudes and values enshrined within them and expressed through
them, and we cannot seriously suppose that God will reject love
and self-giving and the vulnerable meeting of self with the
other, no matter what sexual form it may take.

The corollary of this in relation to the church as Kingdom

community is that if God will not exclude and reject on these grounds, then the church certainly has no possible right to do so. It is, on an entirely different issue, the same question of the church's openness as surfaces from time to time in connection with the granting or withholding of the rites of baptism and marriage. If God is open to all who would approach him then, quite simply, what right has the church to be otherwise than the same?

Secondly, and perhaps of even more immediate and urgent significance, must be the manner in which the ongoing discussion, or conversation to use the language of the previous chapter, is carried on. For however real the disagreements may be, and however sincerely held the various convictions may be, there is quite simply no place in any church which purports, however inadequately, to reflect the Kingdom of God, for the intemperate language (and underlying attitude) of demonisation and denigration which so often characterises the debate.

In an attempt to avoid the use of such language and to find a new starting place for discussion, we have argued here for a fresh departure point for ethics which might henceforth allow us to pursue the conversation in a more 'Kingdom-friendly' manner, and lead us, as we argued at the conclusion of Chapter Eleven, to a renewed conversion and holiness together.

There can be little doubt that, with regard to sexuality, the way forward for the churches in general and for Anglicanism in particular will be a difficult and sometimes painful one, taxing both theology and charity in the highest degree. But this book is written in the hope that, in the sort of approach outlined within it, there is at least a glimmer of light and the possibility of a nearer approach to the Kingdom of God. The hope for the achievement of this lies in the attempt to discover fresh perspectives from which to approach the whole realm of sexuality and especially of sexual ethics, and to offer a way forward which might enable us to resolve (or at least to live charitably with) some of the difficulties and antagonisms with regard to sexuality which are at present so much a feature of the life of the church in all of its forms.

In these pages this attempt has been made, and whilst individual readers (or even whole provinces!) may agree or disagree with the conclusions expressed here, of one thing I am certain: we shall, as a church, or more limitedly as the Anglican Communion, never satisfactorily resolve the issues concerning sexuality and the church while we talk exclusively about ethics. There needs to be – as there has been here – discussion of doctrine, metaphysics, our understanding of the nature of God and of the ways in which we make moral decisions. This book is one contribution to this discussion, to which others will hopefully respond, and it is in these ongoing discussions of these primary things that we shall one day – I hope, and much as I have tried to do here – together find a way forward in the more limited but nonetheless important, evocative and potentially either creative or destructive, healing or pain-inflicting realm of human sexuality.

The Lambeth Commission
and the Windsor Report 2004

The issues addressed in this book have been exercising the minds of many people in the churches recently and not only in the Glenstal Conference which provided the immediate impetus for this volume. Here in Ireland, as we have mentioned, the latest edition of the Church of Ireland journal *Search* was devoted exclusively to the question of homosexuality and the church, and across the Anglican Communion at large the Primates have discussed the matter in the period since Lambeth 1998, and finally in October 2003 requested the Archbishop of Canterbury to form a Commission to explore the issues of communion which have been raised by the actions of the Province of Canada (in particular the Diocese of New Westminster) and the Diocese of New Hampshire.

This book, therefore, has been largely written whilst the Lambeth Commission has been doing its work, and it is being completed just as the commission has published its report, the so-called *Windsor Report*. This report plainly needs to be touched upon in some way here, but a material question arises as to how best to do this. On reflection I have decided to do so by way of this epilogue, and this decision has been reached largely for two reasons. First, it would be awkward and untidy (and superficial) merely to insert references to the report into a pre-existing text; and secondly the report, whilst not changing the substance of this book – but rather, as we shall see, actually reinforcing the need for it – is itself substantially flawed and needs challenging at a number of points, and this is best done in the form of a continuous argument rather than as scattered comments. I propose, therefore, to consider first a number of individual paragraphs in the report, and then secondly to offer a critique of the whole thrust and scope of the report.

At the outset it should be noted that this book is attempting to do precisely what the report calls for but which it itself fails to include. Thus in Paragraph 33 the commission argues that:

> ... neither the Diocese of New Westminster nor the Episcopal Church (USA) has made a serious attempt to offer an explanation to, or consult meaningfully with the Communion as a whole about the significant development of theology which alone could justify the recent moves by a diocese or a province.

Then, a little later, in Paragraph 36 the commission recognises that, '...ethics, liturgy and pastoral practice, if authentically Christian are all rooted in theology and doctrine.' It will be argued later that the failure to make this task (that of the relationship between doctrine and ethics) part of the commission's mandate was a significant and lamentable omission. In the absence of such theological and doctrinal (and indeed ethical) reflection in the *Windsor Report*, this book is at least one attempt to fill this lacuna on behalf of the church.

Turning then to specific aspects of the report, there are a number of places in which one of two errors is committed – either the report is too 'loaded' to be useful or even clear-sighted in its argument, or assumptions are made which are not grounded in any rationale: they are assumed to stand alone as self-evident, but all they actually do when examined more closely is collapse.

The first of these errors surfaces whenever the report is dealing with the attitudes which should be expressed or the actions which might be undertaken by either of the two sides in the homosexuality dispute, and words are applied to one side which could equally well be turned around and applied to the other – and which way round is more appropriate can only finally be decided by addressing the underlying doctrinal and ethical considerations which the report itself does not do. Thus the statements are 'loaded' towards one side of an as yet unresolved debate.

A particularly telling example of this occurs on page 38, paragraph 86 of the report, which states, concerning diversity and new developments that:

> ... any development needs to be explored for its resonance with the truth, and with the utmost charity on the part of all – charity that grants that a new thing can be offered humbly and with integrity, and charity that might refrain from an action which might harm a sister or brother.

On the face of things this appears to be a finely balanced statement in that it suggests attitudes which might be espoused by both parties to the debate. Where it is utterly one-sided, however, is in its conclusion, where the only ones who appear to be capable of being harmed are those who object to a 'new thing'. Yes, such people undoubtedly exist in substantial numbers, but precisely the opposite case could equally well be put: that the refusal to entertain the possibility of a 'new thing' in the case of an issue such as homosexuality is simply continuing to do harm to an equally large (indeed almost certainly larger) number of sisters and brothers. But this is nowhere acknowledged, and the harm which the church has done and is doing to its gay brothers and sisters appears to weigh far less heavily in the scales than the putative harm which might be done to the conservative elements of the church if a more liberal attitude were to be adopted.

Similarly, the Dioceses of New Hampshire and New Westminster are invited to 'regret' their recent actions because of the harm which they have brought to the unity of the Anglican Communion (one suspects, incidentally, that they might both be more than willing to regret the harm, even if not the actions themselves). By the same token, those opposed to their actions might equally well be asked to 'regret' the harm which much intolerant and demonising speech has inflicted on as much as ten per cent of the population. Again no mention is made of this possibility, and the unity of the Anglican Communion appears to be of more significance than the anguish and pain which that Communion continues to inflict on a substantial minority of its members.

It is a curious coincidence that the report's first failing (its sometimes 'loaded' presentation of issues) having surfaced in paragraph 86, that the very next paragraph – and then again in close proximity paragraph 89 – should reveal the second failing, that of unsupported statement and assumption. The first of these paragraphs, number 87, purports to deal with the concept of *adiaphora*, that is, those things which are not central to faith and on which we may therefore safely agree to differ. Behind this lies the question of who decides what things are or are not in this category, and this is a question which the report claims (in paragraphs 90 and following) to address, but which it in fact entirely fails satisfactorily to answer. This failure leaves the discussion precisely where it began, and the invocation of the concept is unclear in its significance. The cases cited are those in Romans and 1 Corinthians 8-10 concerning the eating of food offered to idols, and these are offered as examples of *adiaphora*. However, it should be borne in mind that these things were not *adiaphora* at all to many of the people to whom St Paul was writing: they were central. It was Paul who decided that they were *adiaphora* and history is notoriously written by the winners. What this argument has to say to us now is therefore profoundly unclear: I may conclude that homosexuality comes into the category of *adiaphora* and you may disagree and argue that it is central to faith and doctrine ... and it is only history which will finally prove one or other of us to have been right. But which one? The concept itself is not a useful one for helping us to judge issues which must, in fact, be decided on other grounds entirely, namely those of theology and ethics. *Adiaphora* is a secondary category, and not, as it is presented here, a primary one.

Similarly, in paragraph 89, and still under the general heading of the same discussion, the report addresses the issue of whether some behaviours are self-evidently 'incompatible with inheriting God's coming kingdom, and must not therefore be tolerated within the church'. In principle we may agree that this is the case, but certainly one of the examples invoked is unfortunate and somewhat vitiates the intended idea that the identification of such behaviours is always straightforward. The example is again culled from St Paul, and is that of lawsuits between Christians in non-Christian courts. There are two problems with this. The first is that the report does not (where St Paul himself at least begins to) state why such behaviour is not acceptable: in other words, it is, in the context of the report, an ethical pronouncement which is left hanging in mid-air, and is not, contrary to the report's own stated requirements, rooted in theology and doctrine. The second objection is even more significant. Quite simply we do not, in fact, agree with St Paul any more, which suggests that his pronouncements are not quite as self-evident as is claimed. Paul may have had his own rationale for making these statements in an entirely different culture two thousand years ago, but today we all accept quite happily that both non-Christian and Christian alike will go to law in secular courts. And if we can change our mind on this supposedly self-evident issue, then why not on another?

This absence of theological rationale for stated positions reaches an almost breathtaking climax in paragraphs 125 to 127. It is impossible to discuss these three paragraphs in isolation from one another since it is their juxtaposition which is so revealing, and they are therefore reproduced here in full:

125. There are some areas in which the issue of acceptability is unclear. For example, practice varies across the Communion in relation to divorce and remarriage: there are provinces where it would be unthinkable to appoint a bishop who had been divorced and remarried; there are others where this would be regarded as a secondary issue. The fact of divorce and remarriage would therefore not seem *per se* to be a crucial criterion.

126. There are some matters over which the Communion has expressed its mind. As we have seen, the contentious issue of ordaining women as bishops was the subject of extensive debate and discussion in the Communion for some considerable time before a common mind was reached. After lengthy deliberation, the Instruments of Unity concluded that although the ministry of a woman as bishop might not be accepted in some provinces, that represented a degree of impairment which the Communion could bear.

127. The Communion has also made its collective position clear on the issue of ordaining those who are involved in same gender unions; and this has been reiterated by the primates through their endorsement of the 1998 Lambeth Conference resolution. By electing and confirming such a candidate in the face of the concerns expressed by the wider Communion, the Episcopal Church (USA) has caused deep offence to many faithful Anglican Christians both in its own church and in other parts of the Communion.

Each of these paragraphs simply states that such and such is the case: that is, things are unclear with regard to divorced and remarried bishops, the mind of the communion has been expressed (positively) with regard to female bishops, and expressed (equally negatively) on the subject of the ordination of those involved in same gender unions. We will return to discuss the absence of reasoning in these paragraphs shortly, but it is also worth noting that there are internal inconsistencies here also, especially in connection with paragraph 126. Thus provinces are entitled to disagree on this issue in spite of the fact that the Communion has 'expressed its mind' on the subject, and indeed established that in principle that there is no theological objection to women bishops. If such an entitlement to disagree is the case on one issue, then why not, in principle, on another – unless there is good reason to make a clear distinction between the two cases? If there is not, then it is of dubious integrity to leave one issue open whilst firmly closing another.

The crux of all this, though, is the underlying absence of theological reasoning. It is not explained how or why it is decided which of these issues (divorce and remarriage, female bishops, and the ordination of homosexuals) is more important or why disagreement or diversity should be allowed in some cases but not in others. Divorce, women bishops and the ordination of homosexuals are all equally potentially doctrinal and moral issues, and they cannot readily be discriminated between on these grounds. At the risk of cynicism, it appears that the only substantive difference between them as far as the Anglican

Communion is concerned is, 'How much fuss will be made?' The more the fuss the more theological and moral the issue, apparently!

Finally, in terms of comments on specific paragraphs, the loaded tone of the report re-appears in paragraph 135 – as does a glaringly obvious example of the meaningless double standards so often employed in discussions of homosexuality and ordination. In apparently eirenic manner the paragraph commends the 'listening' process initiated by the 1998 Lambeth Conference, but the trouble is that this 'listening' is to be conducted within a framework (that of the Conference, Primates' Statements and the *Windsor Report* itself) which implies, and indeed occasionally states, that homosexual behaviour is wrong. It is hard to see how within such a framework there can ever be a truly open and receptive listening.

Even worse, however, is the second part of the same paragraph, in which the Episcopal Church (USA) is asked to explain 'how a person living in a same gender union may be considered eligible to lead the flock of Christ'. This betrays the presence of a most appalling double standard which surfaces from time to time in the church's discussions of homosexuality: that is that there should be no distinction made, morally speaking, between leading the flock of Christ and simply being a member of it. What is wrong for clergy is wrong for lay people also, and conversely what is acceptable for lay people must be considered acceptable for clergy also. In this double standard the central issue is lost sight of, and indeed, because of an enduring sense of the cultic mystique of the priesthood and especially the episcopate, actually made more difficult to answer affirmatively. This central issue is that, across the board, either homosexuality is acceptable or it is not. The one option which is not morally defensible is that it should be considered morally right for lay people but morally wrong for a bishop!

These various specific criticisms make it plain that there are a substantial number of confusions and failures which run through the report and which cast doubt on the validity of its

pronouncements. Our final remarks here are, however, addressed to two related and even deeper flaws which underlie
the entire Lambeth Commission process as well as the report itself. The problems with specific sections are substantial, but the
flaws in the whole are crucial.

First, then, the entire thrust of the report (and this is hardly
surprising given its mandate and the constituencies of the vast
majority of its members) puts considerations of practical ecclesiology first, and theology and doctrine firmly second. The overriding concern appears to be with the maintenance of communion rather than with the underlying (and I suggest ultimately
more important) matters of doctrinal, theological and ethical
truth. That this is the case was borne out very recently by an article in the *Irish Times* on 25th October written by the commission's Chairman, the Archbishop of Armagh, which stated
overtly: 'Now Anglicans may well ask how much they are prepared to pay if schism is to be avoided. Does consensus inevitably mean some surrender of truth?'

This is potentially a very slippery and dangerous path. It
may be an extreme example, but the principle involved is well
illustrated by it: what would be the position if, for example,
ninety per cent of the Anglican Communion declared slavery to
be acceptable? Should the other ten per cent accede to this decision for the sake of maintaining communion, or do doctrinal and
moral imperatives override all other considerations – including,
incidentally, the admittedly difficult and regrettable one of the
possibility of inflicting pain on fellow-believers as a result of
one's decision. The primacy of communion is not quite such a
clear-cut, simple or pre-eminent issue as the report appears to
imply, and it also ignores the place of (indeed even the possibility
of) doctrinal, theological or ethical moves of conscience, which it
could be plausibly argued that the actions of New Hampshire
and New Westminster actually are, since they are, in a sense,
freeing (or at least attempting to free) homosexual people from
one particular variety of modern slavery: that of rejection,
exclusion and second class citizenship.

Secondly, and flowing from this, there is the fact that in this almost completely exclusive devotion to ecclesiology, the report only does half a job for the simple reason that the commission was only ever given half a mandate. I am not denying for a moment that the ecclesiological issues and Instruments of Communion needed to be addressed as they are in this report, but the fundamental problem is not that the Lambeth Commission has 'done those things which it ought not to have done' but that it has 'left undone those things which it ought to have done' and has thereby imperilled both its health and its usefulness. For vitally, alongside these matters of communion (certainly at the same time, preferably before and certainly not as an afterthought) there need to be discussed also the equally crucial issues of how we make moral decisions, and how these decisions and the ways in which we make them and the grounds upon which we make them are related to matters of theology and doctrine. There are questions in these disciplines to be re-solved, and that resolution of them will then land Anglicanism in the very uncomfortable position of having no fence to sit upon. In the light of these doctrinal and ethical issues, the Communion will ultimately have to jump one way or the other on the subject of homosexuality, and one of the hardest parts of that jump will be the reluctant acknowledgement that whichever way it is taken will not be without pain – and I suggest that it is at this point that the issues of communion discussed in the *Windsor Report* begin to assume their full importance. Prior to this point, theology and ethics are central, and their substantial omission from the report means that the report appears in some-thing of a vacuum or a limbo. We are now playing theological 'catch up' on matters which require our urgent attention, and the hope must be that in the wake of the report our Communion will be determined enough and strong enough (and prayerful enough) to endure and survive what will need to be a vigorous discussion on these other matters of doctrine and ethics – and in that order. I offer this book as one contribution – and certainly a vigorous one – to that ongoing debate.